MORE THAN JUST HUMMUS

A Gay Jew Discovers Israel in Arabic

MATT ADLER

Editing: Jessica Leving

Publishing and Design Services: MartinPublishingServices.com

ISBN: 978-1-7351546-0-2 (b/w paperback)
         978-1-7351546-2-6 (color paperback
         978-1-7351546-1-9 (e-pub)

CONTENTS

INTRODUCTION

THIS BOOK IS ABOUT MANY THINGS. IT'S ABOUT ADVENTURE. IT'S ABOUT WHAT it's like being a gay man traveling in largely conservative communities in a fairly liberal state. It's about learning what it's like to be an Arab in Israel— and how the Arabic language nourishes the unique character of this country I love and wrestle with.

Most of all, this book is about new things. It's about a suburban gay Reform Jew from Maryland who decided to shake things up in his life and immigrate halfway around the world to his ancestral homeland on July 4, 2017; and in the process, realize that one of his favorite things to do there was to use . . . his Arabic. And write about it.

This book consists of unique stories never before shared on my blog, PlantingRootsBearingFruits.com, as well as blog posts from the site. It's the first time these stories have been collected together under this umbrella theme, and I hope you'll find them entertaining, meaningful, and inspiring. It certainly makes me well up with emotion to share them.

In short, my experience in Israel would not have been what it was, not nearly as emotional or fantastic or eye-opening, without the Arabic language. It's a language that Jews, Muslims, and Christians have spoken for many hundreds of years together. Not always in accord, but always in communication. And it gives me great joy to have taken the Arabic I learned in a college classroom in St. Louis and used it to explore Israel, arguably the best place on the planet to speak the language. A place filled with every dialect imaginable, including some that are no longer found in the Arab world, like Iraqi and Yemenite Judeo-Arabic. These Jewish dialects of Arabic, augmented by the

1

richness of Palestinian dialects, plus the newly-arrived speech of Sudanese refugees, makes Israel a veritable melting pot of the language. It's also by far the safest place in the world for a gay Jew like me to speak the language, which is part of what made it so fun.

I hope that as you read this collection of stories, you'll consider my own situation as I made my way through the process of becoming Israeli. The ideologies I adopted, confronted, and wrestled with. The ones I still believe in and some that I don't. And the many challenges I faced as I dealt with my identity at this time in my life.

This book, while about Arabic and the millions of people who speak it in Israel of many different religions, is not about the Arab-Israeli conflict, although it occasionally touches on it. This is not out of a desire to whitewash problems—I've written about the conflict extensively on my blog from every position imaginable (left, centrist, even occasionally center-right). Rather, it's to say Israel is about so much richness in addition to the conflict, and is worthy of being explored in its own right—in Arabic.

Back living in the States for now, this book makes me nostalgic for my adventures in Israel, my other home. I hope it encourages people to explore the richness of Israel's Arab and Arab-influenced cultures, Jewish, Muslim, Christian, and Druze. And I hope it encourages more Israelis to learn this language which can truly be a cross-cultural bridge.

My hope is that this book brings you closer to your own imagination, and to learning Arabic or whatever language you love and which can nourish you back, bringing you new adventures, new friendships, and new ways of thinking.

Inshallah—may it be so.

ACKNOWLEDGEMENTS

THERE ARE SO MANY PEOPLE I COULD THANK FOR MAKING THESE ADVENTURES possible. Some have names, like my friend Aryeh Solomon who encouraged me to travel in the first place. Finding myself frustrated by an agonizing housing search and adjustment period in Tel Aviv, he told me it was time to step outside the beachside bubble and travel. What started as a trip to Caesarea morphed into a year and a half of wild adventures, only a portion of which are documented in this book. Adventures that gave me a new sense of purpose and life. Thank you Aryeh for your deep friendship and wisdom.

I'd also like to thank my friend Kristle Richardson. It was her idea to start a travel blog in the first place. Without having this outlet, not only would I never have written this book, I would've been much sadder and more disconnected from my friends abroad. What started as a travelogue to keep in touch with them quickly morphed into a way to meet new friends in Israel as well. I owe a tremendous debt of gratitude to Kristle for this suggestion—it changed my life.

I'd also like to thank my mom, Benita Marcus, not only for helping me finance and edit and organize this text, but also for supporting me in taking on the adventure of writing a book. While she wasn't on my journeys themselves, I hope this experience gives her insight into my life at a time when I was far away. Thanks for being there for me when I need you and for being a part of my life.

Thank you to my editor Jessica Leving for helping me bring this text to life—you are a godsend. I'm grateful also to my patient and talented designer Melinda Martin for beautifully arranging my text, photos, and cover.

Then there are the people whose names I don't know but who are no less deserving of my gratitude. For instance, I once found myself hiking in some orchards outside the town of Eilaboun. Parched under the hot Middle Eastern sun, I found myself at risk of dehydration. I came across an old man working in an olive grove. I asked him in Arabic if he had any water. I noticed a large bottle at his side with some small plastic cups. I figured he'd pour me a cup and I'd be on my way. But instead, he picked up the entire bottle and handed it to me. I asked if he was sure—after all, he was working underneath the same scorching sun and was elderly. He insisted. And I downed the bottle of water faster than you could imagine. I can't thank you enough, kind man. You not only saved my health, you inspire me to be a more generous person. That is love.

Whether it was this man in Eilaboun, or the Darfuri refugees whose fruit stand I frequented for lessons about their culture and history, or my Syrian Jewish neighbors who took me in for Shabbat after Shabbat, there are so many people to say "*shukran*" to. Because my adventures in Israel, my adventures in Arabic, wouldn't have been possible or nearly as interesting without you.

Thank you to everyone who has helped me along the way.

Photos used in this collection of essays are courtesy of Matt Adler. Phrases marked with an endnote were originally links in the blog entries. The URLs are provided at the back of the book. Names of some individuals have been changed to protect privacy, but the basic details of the stories are true.

THE NORTH
WHERE MY ARABIC CAN BREATHE

Allahu Akbar—

the time I had that yelled at me and couldn't have been happier

PlantingRootsBearingFruits.com, May 5, 2018

WHO IS WISE? HE WHO LEARNS FROM EVERYONE.

That's what my banner photo says. That's what Rabbi Ben Zuma said 2,000 years ago.

Did I find this in Bnei Brak or Jerusalem? No. I found it in a Druze[1] village—Yanuh—with a Jewish population of 0. An absolutely gorgeous place with stunning greenery all around. Super friendly people. And—at least when I was there—not a single tourist. Due to my clothing and my fabulous blue sunglasses, everyone knew I was from out of town.

And when I opened my mouth to speak Arabic, the smiles were constant. The laughter, the joy, the jokes—jokes with me. Because I can speak to them in their native tongue. I am a polyglot—I speak eight languages fluently or proficiently. I have an "ear" for language, undoubtedly, but I also use them. A lot. I don't memorize vocabulary on my phone—I hang out in Druze villages. I talk to cab drivers in Arabic. The other day I got my friend a discount on strawberries at the market in my Jewish neighborhood because the Arab vendor was so excited that I spoke Arabic.

Why would Arabic speakers here be so excited to hear me speak it? I can think of a few reasons. For me, it honestly just feels natural. I love speaking Arabic. And unfortunately, due to the extremists trying to tear down the border fence in Gaza to "liberate" my neighborhood, I've felt further and further from the language. When certain Palestinians decide to fly burning kites[2] over the border fence to set my country's farms on fire, I have a hard time connecting to the language they speak.

Which reminded me—not only Palestinians speak Arabic. A lot of times, the news media and even leftist Israelis who choose to learn the language are exclusively focused on Palestinians. It's not a bad thing to want to dialogue with them—the more people learning languages the better. In all societies, especially here.

It's just that Palestinians are not our only neighbors. Certainly not our only neighbors who speak Arabic. About 20% of the Israeli population—citizens—speak Arabic as a first language. And lucky for me, the Arabic-speakers up north, in the Galilee and Golan, speak the dialects closest to mine. Syrian.

Why do I speak Syrian Arabic? Besides the fact that it, perhaps alongside Lebanese, is in my opinion the most beautiful Arabic dialect, it was a bit due to circumstance. At my university, I studied *Fusha*, Modern Standard Arabic (more of a literary language). Only after 3 years did I have the chance to learn *ammiyya*, or spoken Arabic. I had the choice of Egyptian or Syrian, and I chose the latter because it was mutually intelligible with Palestinian. And I also care about dialogue. My professor was from Damascus. He was homophobic and somewhat anti-Semitic, but his Arabic was astounding and I learned so much.

Since then, Syria was plunged into civil war and I never got the chance to visit. Though, along with Lebanon, it would be my dream to do so. *Inshallah*—God Willing. In the meantime, the closest thing I can get to speaking my Damascus Arabic is to simply hop on a bus up north. Or speak with my Syrian refugee friends, which I do each week.[3]

The Druze, in particular, migrated to northern Israel over the past 800 years. From Aleppo, Lebanon, and beyond. Of course, the Druze in the Golan Heights were living in Syria just 50 years ago, so their Arabic is very close to mine too.

And to a person, everyone is excited to hear me speaking their language. And their dialect. Not Palestinian Arabic—Syrian Arabic. Quite often, people actually ask me if I'm Lebanese or Syrian. The most flattering thing I've ever heard.

Today the coolest thing happened. I was visiting Isfiya, a Druze village with significant Christian and Muslim minorities. After visiting a Bedouin shop and some churches (the Christian dialects up here are also super close to my own and fun to hear), I had dinner at a Druze grocery store. Yes, because the grocery store also doubled as a roadside food stand with kebabs. I love my country.

While my kebabs were roasting, I popped over to the cell phone shop. I wanted to buy a portable phone charger so I can travel at ease and get some extra juice when I need it. I initially approached the young man in Hebrew. And then, just like every Arab and Druze person does here millions of times a day, I slipped into Arabic. Five Arabic words here, one Hebrew word there—it's the most beautiful and fun thing. Kind of an Arabic Yiddish with amazing wordplay. A young kid said to me today: *"Ani rotzeh she***'anjah***"*. I want to win. The italics Hebrew, the bold Arabic, and it flowed perfectly as we giggled at the combination. It's fun when you can enjoy the best of each other's cultures. To the point where they're hummus and tehina. You can't fully separate them and they're delicious together.

So I'm at the phone store and my Arabic starts flowing and a Druze man, no more than 20 years old, lets out an "Allahu Akbar!" to shake the ground. In such shock and delight at seeing a Jewish American-Israeli speaking his language, he simply praised God.

I had this deep inner sense of joy and satisfaction. I felt so, so complimented. It was funny. It was sweet. It was sincere. And it was a beautiful way to take a phrase that radical Islamic terrorists use to blow people like me up—and instead use it to bring us together in unity. In a cell phone store. It tickled me.

This kind of reaction happens to me a lot, especially up north. When I tell some of my Israeli Jewish friends about the villages I've visited, a good number of them have never even been. Or in some cases, even heard of them. Or even think they're worth visiting. It's not universal—I've hitchhiked with Jews who were visiting these villages. But it's an extreme, extreme minority. Jews here do not speak Arabic. Other than older generations of Jews from Middle Eastern countries and a few dedicated young people who paid attention in school (or the army), Jews don't care to learn Arabic here.

It makes me sad. On a few levels. One, because I understand why. There is a 70-year-old trauma-inducing conflict here, separate educational systems for Jews and Arabic-speakers, and largely separate residential patterns. And while there are people in both societies who want to mix, overall there is a desire to retain communal identities. Which can make it hard to learn each other's languages. Especially Arabic, whose spoken varieties aren't standard-ized and really require in-person experiences.

And yet, only about 10% of Jews here speak Arabic but 77% of Arab Israelis[4] speak Hebrew. About 29% of Arabs here can't read Hebrew—which is an issue for employment, social cohesion, and communication. But let's just say Arab citizens of Israel are way, way more invested in learning Hebrew than vice-versa. Which is a national *shanda*. That's Yiddish for scandal.

While this may be par for the course for majority-minority relations (after all, how many non-Latino Americans speak Spanish? Answer: about 10%[5], the same as Jewish Israelis with Arabic), it's not acceptable. While I value the smiles I get from young Druze and Christian Arabs and even Muslim kids (in those villages I feel are safe enough to visit, which is not all of them), I don't want to be an oddity. I want more of my countrymen to stop whining and pick up a book. Take a class. Visit your neighboring village.

Arabic speakers in Israel are almost universally happy to help. And eager to see you give a shit. I don't really care how many times you voted for Meretz or how you do a once-a-year interfaith Seder. Stop being a lazy (fill in the blank with something that will motivate you) and get to work! If you spent half as much time learning Arabic as you did complaining about your salad dressing, you'd be fluent. Arabic takes practice but it's so much fun! It will take you on new adventures—musically, socially, geographically, historically, and beyond. It's a true civilization.

And the good news is that even when some people who speak the lan-guage are becoming increasingly extremist, you can find great places in Israel to practice the language safely. Basically, any Druze or Christian village, most Bedouin towns, and even some other Muslim villages like Abu Ghosh. Or beyond, when the conditions are right. I've traveled in some deeply conservative Muslim villages and had some close calls safety-wise—so I can understand if you don't want to start there. The vast majority of people I've met in all places were cool. It is true that it just takes one nut-job to end your life. So do some research if you want to go far off the beaten path.

In the end, the North of Israel is the best. It's the place where I dabke dance on the street with Druze kids, where I counseled a bi-curious young man[6] in Arabic, and where I get private tours of churches followed by tons of homemade pastries. It's a land of generosity, of green hills, of smiles.

When I leave a Druze village, a place where my Judaism and my Israeliness and my Arabic-speaking identity are all validated, I hate getting on the bus. Tel Aviv is a vibrant, energetic, queer-friendly coastal city. With a beach. There are things here that are unique and maybe it made sense for me to start here.

But as I spend more time in other parts of the country, especially the North, I wonder if Tel Aviv will really be home for me. Maybe I'll split my time (perhaps people up north will want to trade apartments once in a while ☺). Maybe I'll live here but keep traveling a lot. Maybe I'll just move up north.

What I do know is this: Tel Aviv smells terrible. And when I hop off the bus, the stench is overwhelming, the noise is loud, the nature is nonexistent. Yes, there are exceptions. There are beautiful areas near me just south of the city.

But would I rather have a late-night pizza place, or make some at home and sit in a forest and stare at the stars in awe?

Where my Arabic and my soul can breathe.

THE BI-CURIOUS DRUZE BOY

To protect the young person involved, no names or identifying information is used in this story, but all the essential details are true.

PlantingRootsBearingFruits.com, May 1, 2018

THE PAST FEW DAYS, I WENT ON A TRIP TO WHAT I CALL THE DRUZE GALILEE. There's an area largely north of Karmiel where there's Druze village after Druze village and they're all absolutely gorgeous. Here are some pretty pictures:

It's a beautiful, peaceful place where I enjoyed practicing my Arabic. I love speaking Arabic, but due to fanaticism among some sectors of society, I can't speak it comfortably everywhere— especially as a Jew and as an Israeli (and sometimes even an American). What's great about Druze villages is they, by and large, wholeheartedly accept me as a Jewish Israeli and are thrilled to see a Jew taking interest in their language and culture.

Early in my trip, I was walking up a hill and a young man, 17 almost 18 years old, pulled over his moped and said hi. As with all my stories from this trip, pretty much everything was in Arabic with a sprinkling of Hebrew. He asked where I was going and offered to get me in the right direction. So I hopped on with him and he drove.

I felt free, riding around in the countryside, babbling in Arabic as the wind swept across my face. A young Druze boy showing me around his beautiful neck of the woods. Couldn't get better. I asked him to pull over to take some pictures. He begged me not to get off—"We could go for a trip!" I asked him to wait a second as I took some pictures. Because suddenly there were goats in the way! Tons and tons of goats! I was so excited—having spent most of my life in cities, it was pretty exciting to see goats on the road!

While I took pictures of the goats, the young man started asking me questions—questions I often get from young Arab kids here: "Do you have a girlfriend or boyfriend in Tel Aviv?" I said no. "But if you had one, would it be a boyfriend or girlfriend?" he asked with hesitation. "Boyfriend," I said. "Boyfriend? Like male or female? Or like the ones who change their gender?" "Nope, just a boyfriend. A man and a man together."

I waited for the reaction. It was a gamble on my part. We were pretty much alone on a wooded path at least 100 meters from a main street. I knew absolutely nobody in the area. He had a moped and I had…a cellphone? In the end, you don't know how people will react. Druze, while extraordinarily accepting of my Judaism, are known for being quite socially conservative, including on gay issues. Not like certain right-wing Christians in the U.S. who try to influence the law because of it, but conservative nonetheless. And I was the only Israeli Jew for several miles around. I had never been to this part of Israel.

Trusting my good instincts and what seemed to be his good nature, I stood there with him, next to his moped. And it turned out, I not only made a good choice, I may have done a mitzvah. A good deed. He continued to ask me all sorts of questions about gay people and my life. Dating, romance, sex, even the wild world of the Internet. Of course, some things I just wasn't comfortable sharing—to respect my privacy and because, remember, he was 17 years old. But I did share what I thought was relevant and helpful and appropriate.

After the 20th question, I asked him: "Are you asking me these questions because you yourself are curious?" And he said: "Maybe…could we do something?"

I smiled. On some level, I was flattered. Also intrigued that this guy knew I was gay simply by meeting me on the street. And that he had a comfort level to ask me these (sometimes invasive but well-intentioned) questions. We had a nice moment. It makes me smile to think a Druze teenager propositioned me. Seventeen-year-old me would've loved such a moment. If I hadn't been being abused by some family members and subjected to rabid homophobia at school, in sports, and even sometimes in synagogue—I would've come out sooner, and maybe I could've had more high school romances. Maybe even with a Druze guy!

But the reality was that I was 32 and he was a minor. I wanted to be supportive of his desire to learn more, and also had to draw some clear limits. I explained to him why we couldn't have sex and he was disappointed. He said: "There are other guys in the village—they have sex with men, but I'm not sure they're gay. If I have sex with a man, does it mean I'm gay?"

I told him: "You have to discover that for yourself. Some people try things and it's more of an experience. Some people feel it fits them. It's up to you."

I thought back to an earlier part of our conversation when he asked me how I knew I was gay. I've gotten this question millions of times from liberal Americans and it frustrates the hell out of me. Nobody asks them how they figured out they were straight. Because it's something you feel, it's not something you wake up in the morning and decide. The only reason we have to discover it is because society assumes we're not gay from the day we're born. And we have to uncover an identity hidden from us, that nobody will bestow upon us. After what is often years of estrangement, many (though not all) of us come to realize who we are and what we like. It can be exhausting and quite hard.

Before I realized this young man was curious about his own identity, I had told him: "Well, I know I'm gay just like you know you're straight. You just are. How did you know you were straight?"

And then I realized: he didn't know. And he may never know.

This young man was not any old Druze. He was a religious Druze. There are secular and religious Druze—the latter take on many more responsibilities along with special dress and customs. He'd dated girls some and seemed to like it—I'm not sure to what extent. If he lived in a more liberal society, perhaps he'd be out by now. I don't know. Maybe he's bi. Maybe he's gay. Maybe he's straight and just trying things out. I don't know. And I hope, even with the pressures of the society around him—a society I love dearly—that he can figure out the best path forward for him.

If that means coming out and risking family disapproval or being cut off—I wish him well. He did mention one family in the village that had a gay son living elsewhere in Israel with a boyfriend— and the family accepted the two of them. That's pretty awesome. Maybe my friend will get married and have trysts (or maybe not). I hope he's happy. I'm not here to judge him. It's hard to straddle multiple identities—and in the case of being Druze and (maybe) gay—it must be even more difficult. You shouldn't have to give up one part of yourself to be another. And the reality is negotiating that balance, as hard as it is, might be worth it. I pray for his well-being and his happiness.

I saw the disappointment on his face when I said no to a romantic tryst in the woods (but readers, I *am* single—so if you're of age, I do like the idea of kissing under a cedar 😊). I bid him goodbye with this blessing: "Good luck *habibi, bnjaah*! Find someone your age 😊. It'll be okay."

He smiled as he went down the mountain on his moped. Teenage me was smiling. I hope I did for him what I wish more people had done for me at his age.

My milkshake brings all the Druze to the yard. Now if only I can find one my own age… 😊

SOUTH TEL AVIV IS
THE BEST TEL AVIV

Arabic Shabbat:

when you realize your Jewish neighbors speak Arabic . . .

as a native language

PlantingRootsBearingFruits.com, November 19, 2017

After a long and arduous search, I finally found a long-term apartment! Everything about my identity—being Reform, being American, being progressive, and being queer—should lead me to live in the more secular center and north of the city. But I feel utterly blessed that I ended up in the south.

When I first moved to my neighborhood, the border of Yad Eliyahu and Shchunat Hatikvah, I was apprehensive. I knew absolutely no one there and there were posters advertising Shas[7] concerts everywhere. There are almost no young secular/Reform Ashkenazi people in this neighborhood, and I have yet to see a pride flag. There are no pubs, nightclubs, cafes with WiFi—it is quiet. Part of that is the beauty of the place and why I chose to live there. Though at times, it was so quiet I felt lonely.

Today, a few weeks after move-in day, I had no plans for Shabbat. I had plans Saturday night, but during the day I figured I'd wander around and get to know my neighborhood. And then I heard a boom. And a tap tap. Boom. And a tap tap…it was a darbuka[8]! I stepped outside and heard loud clapping and drumming and singing coming from across the street. Not the utterly depressing slow moan of westernized Israeli rock (sorry guys—I do like some of it, but mostly it makes me want to cry!). But rather the boom boom and ululating of Middle Eastern music.

I'm an outgoing guy, so I simply stood outside and listened—and as seems to be the Israeli custom, they immediately invited me inside. When I say invited—I don't mean a polite "how do you do?" and offering a cup of tea. No—I was ushered into a room of 20 people, given a Mexican sombrero, plied with food and drink, all while I danced with people I just met to beautiful, soul-stirring Mizrachi music[9].

It was amazing and overwhelming all at the same time. While I danced, the uncle tried to get me to drink whiskey (I don't drink), then the cousin handed me pitas with hot dogs in them (which I shook while I danced), then the grandfather told me over and over again to keep eating! I was living my dream of being in My Big Fat Greek Wedding[10].

Then, the most amazing thing happened. The family asked me what song I'd like to sing. I am an avid Mizrachi music fan. This music is, hands down, the most unique cultural product to ever come out of Israel, although many (sometimes racist) Israelis wouldn't realize that. This music was born out of a fusion of the traditional Arabic, Turkish, Greek, Ladino, and Persian music brought by Jews to Israel in the 40s and 50s. It then used the best of the West—drum sets, synthesizers, and electric guitars to imitate traditional instruments. Add in a dose of Israeli folk tunes along with elements of Ashkenazi[11] melodies and voila, you have the first "world music" before "world music" even existed!

So as I stood there, the first song that came to mind was "Mabruk Aleek". It's an Arabic-language wedding song. And there I was dancing, having an absolute blast. As with most things in Israel, life can go from quiet and lonely to exciting and heart-warming in a matter of seconds.

I was told I could sit and eat now, as relative after relative brought me food and water and food and water. But things only got better—I discovered my new adoptive family is half Syrian and half Iraqi. And with the exception of the youngest generation, everyone in the room speaks Arabic! I specifically studied Syrian Arabic in college in the U.S. with a professor from Damascus—and now with Syrian refugees on Skype[12]. It was a dream come true! Everyone smiling with each Arabic word I say. Spending Shabbat with Jews—in Arabic!! For an American Ashkenazi Jew, this was a surreal experience, and one I'll never forget (though I've been invited to come again over and over, so I doubt it'll be the last!).

Then we moved to another room so I could meet the other 15 relatives. I was asked at least three or four times if I was married, but the final time it was because they wanted to set me up with someone's daughter. The first few times I laughed off the question, but now I had a choice to make. In the living room where we were banging on darbukas and recording videos on cell phones (things Orthodox Ashkenazi Jews don't do on Shabbat), there were also at least half a dozen pictures of a rabbi who I presume was Rav Ovadia[13], who founded the Haredi Shas party. Let's just say the party isn't generally a big fan of gays, Reform Jews, or really most of the things that people in the north of Tel Aviv support.

So, I debated internally and did something brave: "You can set me up with her daughter, but it won't work because I'm gay." I looked around and asked: "Are you in shock?" And without skipping a beat, one of the aunts said to me: "Oh no, we have that in our family too." I started to smile as relative after relative started thinking of men to set me up with. One of the younger relatives actually pulled out her phone, called her friend, and got me the number of a gay guy to help me make friends in the community.

After helping one of the men download an app on his phone to turn YouTube videos into MP3s (he loves everything from Eyal Golan to Umm Kulthum[14]), I hung out with the youngest kids—two 10-year-old girls. We danced to Justin Bieber on the street and made funny videos.

Before I left, I was of course given a full container of homemade Iraqi kubbeh[15] and rice. They told me to come by whenever and one of the little girls even said, "come every Shabbat!" at least three times. They took my number and said they'd introduce me to the neighbors, show me where I can volunteer, and feed me a lot.

My neighborhood is a lot browner, a lot more Middle Eastern, a lot more Arabic-speaking, and a lot more working-class than North Tel Aviv. And you know what? That's not only "OK" by me—it's fucking amazing. Because the 14-year-old me who went by himself to a Sarit Hadad[16] concert in Maryland is smiling from ear to ear. Mizrachi music—Mizrachi culture— isn't something new for me. It's something that, from the first days of when I learned Modern Hebrew after my Bar Mitzvah, gave me hope in dark times and energy and smiles. It connected me to my Judaism and to Israel itself.

Unfortunately, there are many Israelis now and back in the early days of the State who are avidly racist against Mizrachim[17]. Even Mizrachi music was banned from the radio by the government in its early days. And to the surprise perhaps of some of my fellow progressive American Jewish friends, this racism largely comes from secularized "progressive" Jews of Ashkenazi origin. The kind who write for Haaretz or sit[18] on the Supreme Court—two of our favorite institutions.

But let's move beyond the politics. What I'm trying to say is, my neighborhood—this is not where the tourists are. This is not where the wealthy people are. This is not "trendy" and it's not French-Vietnamese vegan fusion food. These are people who have fought for their cultural and economic existence and are here to tell the tale. These are people whose Sephardic Judaism has a remarkable fluidity—even queerness—to it.

God bless them. Because when a lonely, newly-minted Israeli stumbled outside his house today, he didn't just meet his neighbors. He met family.

Because for all the beautiful luxury penthouses in North Tel Aviv, there's one thing money can't buy.

Warmth.

HAREDIM SPEAKING ARABIC, DABKE, AND AIR RAID SIRENS

Black Hats and Arabic—
the ultra-Orthodox Jews who speak the tongue of Muhammad

PlantingRootsBearingFruits.com, November 2, 2017

Yesterday, I was sitting on a bus. In front of me, there were two Haredim[19], a man in a black hat and his wife. But they weren't speaking Yiddish—they were speaking Arabic!

I listened closely to make sure it wasn't just Hebrew with a Mizrachi[20] accent, but no, sure enough it was Arabic. I then, in a first for me, spoke to Haredim in Arabic. Turns out the man had been born in Egypt and moved to Israel at a very young age. And his wife Miriam—now this is interesting—is Jordanian. And, in her words, Arab. Very, very few Mizrachim would identify as Arab—especially today, but even historically—many were simply Jews who lived in relative peace among their Muslim and Christian neighbors.

The chaos of the modern era changed that, before nationalism, including pan-Arab nationalism (or modern Zionism) existed.

Therefore, given that a Mizrachi Jew, even who speaks some variety of Arabic or Judeo-Arabic, would likely not identify as an Arab, I wondered about this woman. Just a few days before, I had been reading about Jordan and while it has a rich ancient Jewish history, it hasn't had a stable Jewish community for quite a long time.

Which got me thinking—I believe Miriam is a convert. In her own words, she is proud of being Arab and thinks there are good Arabs, Jews—good everyone everywhere. But she thinks Jews are nicer than Arabs. I responded that I wasn't so sure based on my interactions with real estate agents here! We laughed.

Before I got off the bus, we passed by what I presume was a left-wing demonstration. Yesterday was the anniversary of the assassination of Yitzhak Rabin[21], the former Prime Minister of Israel. He had tried to forge a peace agreement with the Palestinians and was murdered by a fanatical right-wing Jew. The protestors blocked the intersection and started slapping the bus. I was kind of concerned, but mostly I was pissed off that these people were keeping me from my destination. I'm all for peace demonstrations, but I'm not sure what you accomplish by scaring a bunch of innocent people on a bus. I once thought only right-wing people could be fanatical, but I've found that people of any political stripe can be utterly intolerant and invalidating.

Annoyed by the demonstrators and extremely excited about the Haredi Arabic conversation I'd just had, I hopped off the bus and headed north to a *dabke* workshop. Dabke[22] is a traditional Levantine dance popular among Palestinians, Jordanians, Lebanese, Syrians, Kurds, and Iraqis. For years, I've loved this dance. It just looks so fun! I've watched YouTube clips and listened to the music on my iPod. In Arabic class in college, we got a brief introduction to it, but I never really had the chance to dance it.

Until last night. I found an amazing workshop and danced my pants off. It was so much fun and the people there were at least as fun as the dance. Being the only Jew—the only non-Arab—in the room, I aroused a lot of curiosity. And frankly, mostly a bunch of friendliness. People gave me their numbers, invited me to hang out with them, asked me about America and even Israeli folk dancing (which I also do). I even met two separate women who wanted to practice Spanish with me! And the whole session—before you ask if you can join me—is in Arabic. This is their space, as it should be, and they were generous enough to allow me to enter it and enjoy their culture. So unless you've got some pretty strong Arabic, you're going to have to take a language class before you take the dance class. ☺

If you want to take a look, this video[23] is what our dance looked like last night! (I'm the guy in the blue shorts and teal shirt). So much fun!

I returned home feeling buoyant. As I got ready for bed, I started hearing a loud noise. This was my first night in a new apartment, so I thought it might be the sirens from the hospital nearby. And then I heard what sounded like airplanes. Getting louder and louder.

My first thought was that my landlord ripped me off by giving me an affordable apartment that constantly has flyovers from Ben Gurion Airport. What a jerk!

But then I realized—the sirens kept going. This isn't an ambulance. This isn't a plane. This is an air raid siren.

Having absolutely no idea what to do in this situation (luckily, I'd never experienced it in America), I googled it. And thank God somebody had taken the time to write it. Go to the ground floor, avoid windows and doors, and pray. And at 3:30 a.m., that's exactly what I did. Alone and in the dark.

I was scared absolutely shitless. I prayed and prayed and messaged a couple friends who were equally confused. After a while (which seemed like a very long while), the news published that it was a false alarm. But I'll tell you, it didn't sound so false when I heard plane (projectile?) after plane (missile?) overhead over and over again. I envisioned my building collapsing to the ground. Would I survive?

Thank God I did and thank God everyone is okay. I've truly never experienced something like that in my life before. And I hope you don't either—it's scary. And having read that earlier today, the terrorist group Islamic Jihad was threatening revenge because Israel destroyed one of their weapons smuggling tunnels… And that there was an armed confrontation between Israel and Syria in the north . . . It wouldn't have been a shock if the air raid sirens had been accurate.

Being someone who has already suffered trauma in my life, it was hard to get to sleep—it pushed a whole bunch of triggers. Finally I was able to lie down and get some rest.

I wrote to my friends on Facebook last night that if you don't have the dedication and faith to keep you here, you simply won't make it.

Everyone has a stake in this society and we must work together to make it the best place on the planet—which I think it is and has the potential to be.

I understand the rage that people can feel here—when you're scared, when you're scarred, you just want to lash out. There are productive ways to do this and harmful ones and I hope we can strive to do the former more than the latter.

To anyone outside of Israel who has any doubt as to what terrorism does to the Israeli psyche, I invite you to crash at my place next time there's an air raid siren. All the Ambien in the world won't help you sleep and it will haunt you after you wake.

And to the "peace" activists who slapped my bus—I get you. You're horrified, you've been hurt by someone, somewhere in this Holy Land. But get a therapist. Do some yoga. Pray. Take some anti-anxiety medications. Whatever works for you. But stop taking out your anger on your fellow man.

Be like the hundreds of young people I saw engaging in dialogue in Kikar Rabin[24] yesterday. Be like the Haredi man who married a Jordanian (convert?) and speaks Arabic. Be like me and go dance Palestinian dabke with new Arab friends.

Or be like my Arab friend Lena who I met last night. When I told her I was an American Jew who now lived in Tel Aviv, her answer was simple and touching:

"You are welcome here."

That, my friends, is how you make peace. One heart at a time. A quiet and beautiful answer to the screeching of a siren.

As my banner photo says in Arabic: "Life is sweet." Damn straight it is. Because I'm alive.

A MUSLIM PLURALIST

A Visit to the Arab Triangle—
exploring the least touristy and most authentic side of Arab Israel, Tira

PlantingRootsBearingFruits.com, March 31, 2018

ONE OF THE GREAT FRUSTRATIONS I'VE FACED WHEN DEALING WITH DIALOGUE here is that some people aren't pluralists. Being a pluralist, as I see it, is about saying "I have one way of doing things, you have another, let's co-exist." It means legally allowing people to do things you don't agree with. It's not about getting into a war of whose tradition is better, it's just accepting that we're all in this together with some right to autonomy.

In the Jewish World, this is a frequent dilemma. There are Orthodox Jews who see Reform Jews as inadequately Jewish (hence why my movement is not recognized by the Israeli government). There are secular Jews who think Orthodox Jews are overly superstitious, conservative, and backwards and should just modernize with the times. While in the U.S. Jewish pluralism is stronger than in Israel (perhaps because it's not tied up with a government), there are still issues in communities across the pond.

That being said, you can't even begin to compare American pluralism with what goes on in Israel. Here, there is no separation of Church/Synagogue/Mosque and State. Which means progressive Jewish movements are put at a disadvantage[25] financially, legally, and politically. The same could be said for people who feel Jewish and aren't recognized as such and also people who just aren't religious at all. Of any background.

I find that communities here struggle—on all sides—with the idea of letting someone else do something you disagree with. You'll find militant vegans protesting Hasidic[26] kapores[27] rituals but not protesting the hamburger joint on their block. You'll find Reform Jews railing against Hasidic intolerance, while making fun of their clothes, their language, and their religiosity. If you replace Hasidic with Hispanic, I doubt my fellow Reform Jews would make fun of their culture. Of course you also have the more well-known bigotry of Haredim[28] who throw stones at cars and "immodest" women, etc. etc.

These circles of intolerance extend to other religions here. I've met Greek Orthodox Christians who claim they came before the Catholics. I've met Catholics who railed against Evangelicals. I've met Evangelicals who told me I'm not being a good *Jew*. I've met Muslims who said Arabic was the world's first language, as uttered by God. And couldn't believe I didn't convert to Islam after reading the Quran. I've met Arab Christians who don't particularly like Muslims. And Arab Muslims who don't believe Jews have any connection to this place—and told me this to my face. And I've met Arab Muslims who get ridiculed by other Arab Muslims for being half-Romanian or immodest or even for being Bedouin.

And of course, you have the Palestinians who want to wipe Israeli Jews off "their land". And the Israeli Jews who don't recognize that Palestinians even exist

It's enough to make your head spin. Probably like yours is now.

So at times like these, when people here just fill you with sadness and anger, I like to think of strong counterexamples. At a time when Islam is turning increasingly fundamentalist—or at least, its fundamentalist elements are growing in prominence—I met the most unlikely Muslim pluralist.

I was in the Arab village of Tira. There, I met a high school student named Jamila. She worked at the local toy store. I had never been to an Arab toy store, so I wanted to see what it looked like.

She was super-sweet. While I came in trying to show my deference to her culture, all she wanted to talk about was Israeli and American culture. She really wants to visit Tel Aviv more. She loves American movies. Hebrew is her favorite subject, Harry Potter—not the Quran—her favorite book. Nothing wrong with liking the Quran—I personally love parts of it. Just that Jamila is not who you might expect to say this.

Because Jamila wears a hijab. A headscarf. Generally a sign of religious conservatism or perhaps devotion to tradition. And a bone of serious contention in Western Europe[29].

When she kept talking about how much she liked Jewish culture here, I asked why. Her answer contains a grain of truth we all should pay attention to.

She said: "What I really like is that when you go to the beach here, the Jewish women can wear whatever they want."

Before you launch into a Western-style approbation of hijabs, that's not what's going on here.

I asked her: "So you mean you wish you didn't have to wear a hijab?" After all, I have met Arab girls here who have told me that.

She said: "No, I wear a hijab because that's my tradition. I'm Muslim. What I like is that they don't *have to*. The Jewish women have the choice. I like riding my bike, but some people here don't approve because I'm a woman."

In other words, Jamila is a pretty awesome example of a pluralist. She wears a hijab—and would continue to do so—she just likes that Jews here tend to have more choice. That she could wear a hijab but maybe her sister wouldn't. Or would change her mind according to her views over time.

Jamila, surprisingly, is a good example for all of us. We do not have to agree on many things. I admire the Hasidic community for keeping Yiddish alive, for preserving certain customs, and for their birthrate, to be honest. I see other things in the community, such as homophobia or gender politics, as quite problematic. And people ask me: "Well Matt, you're a queer Reform Jew, how could you possibly like Hasidim? They won't accept you."

To which I say: "I'm a pluralist." I can like what I like about certain communities and not like what I don't like. I can accept that both aspects exist. And I'm entitled to my feelings on them. Unlike some of the more militant secularists here, I don't want Haredim to abandon their traditions because they're "backwards". I do want more of a separation of religion and state. And there are things I like about their community. The things I don't—well, sometimes you have to find other avenues for making your case rather than imposing laws. And—this is the tough one for many people—sometimes you just acknowledge that it's there, whether you agree or not. And that it's maybe not my role to change everything about how someone else lives.

Like Jamila and her hijab, I don't want everyone to be like me. I want people to be free to choose their own path, even when I don't want to follow it. It's important to remember coercion can flow in all directions, left and right. Muslim and Christian. Orthodox, Reform, and Secular. Israeli and

Palestinian. My respect for conservative traditions is not necessarily at the expense of my progressive values.

Lehefech, as we say in Hebrew. "To the contrary". It is because of them.

COMING OUT TO
A (HOT STRAIGHT) ARAB
CATHOLIC GUY...IN ARABIC!

PlantingRootsBearingFruits.com October 13, 2017

Okay so I'm going to make you wait a bit to get to the title story, but we'll get there soon. 😊 First, I want to tell you about Tarshiha.

I decided to wander around the Arab village of Tarshiha alone. Having talked to several Jewish Sabras[30] here afterwards, they were a bit surprised— and none of them had done it themselves. This seemed bizarre to me— Tarshiha, half of the mixed Jewish-Arab municipality of Ma'alot Tarshiha[31], felt much, much safer than at least half of my hometown of D.C. And it's historic and beautiful.

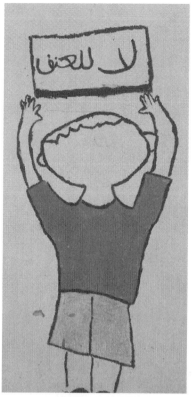

As I like to do, I wandered around with pretty much no agenda other than exploring and meeting cool people. And speaking a ton of Arabic. 😊 As my new favorite self-made motto goes: "If you're cool, I'm down."

Among a bunch of historic homes, I noticed a door that said "Photography Studio". I talked to the man inside, a 30-year-old named Eli (short for Elias). He is indeed a photographer and he invited me into his studio and immediately made me Arab coffee (think shot-sized coffee and much, much stronger). Because that's how things work here.

Since I happen to do social media public relations for a living, he asked me some questions about Facebook. I sat down with him for about an hour and showed him tricks of the trade, because why the hell not? He's a good guy. Plus his *Fusha* (Modern Standard Arabic, for writing) was a little rusty, so I helped him add a section on his page in Arabic. Otherwise, he had written his page information, geared towards Arab clientele (weddings, etc.)—in Hebrew! Somebody go write a PhD thesis about the American Jewish *oleh* helping an Arab-Israeli write in Arabic because he was publicizing his events to Arabs…in Hebrew. Unpack that for a lifetime! So much meaning here. 😊

As we sat and sipped our drinks, car after car of his relatives pulled up by the door and everyone greeted each other. A cousin was a famous journalist, an uncle was a (Arab Greek Orthodox Christian) Mizrachi[32] singer who performs for the Iraqi and Kurdish Jews in the neighboring villages (again—PhD thesis material). I could go on and on, but this town was like a non-stop family reunion. I felt like it was *My Big Fat Greek Wedding* but an entire village. And I loved it.

Before making my way to another part of town, we exchanged contact info. He showed me his newly renovated church around the corner with great pride (even though he identified as "Secular Orthodox"—a hilarious phrase in a Jewish context). Then he did something extraordinary. This man knew I was an *oleh chadash* and that I knew very few people in Israel. He pointed his hand towards the door of the studio and said in Hebrew: "*Tireh, bo matay sheba lecha. Zeh habayit shelcha.*" Come whenever you want. This is your home.

I came to Israel looking for family. I just didn't expect it would be a Secular Greek Orthodox Arab man! But why the hell not? I can't think of a more generous way to welcome me to Israel than what he said. And you better believe I'll be back—especially for the weddings he photographs!

I continued to wander about the village. Most people were welcoming—a few stared. I don't think many Jews wander the residential neighborhoods of Tarshiha, so I might have looked like a bit of an oddity. But frankly, I was proud of myself for trying something new and I met a lot of kind and welcoming people there. I find it absolutely embarrassing that not a small number of my fellow Jewish Israelis know more about South America, Germany, or India than about their own neighbors. It's not only problematic for the future of this country, it's also a great loss for the people who don't visit. I literally stumbled upon an Ottoman mosque and administrative headquarters just when looking for a bathroom. It's true that it can be scary or disorienting to get lost in an unfamiliar town, but if you can handle trekking in the Himalayas, you probably have the instincts to manage Tarshiha.

Out of the corner of my eye, I caught sight of a door and house covered in flowers. It was gorgeous. Clearly someone had put great effort into making it pretty. There was a picture of a woman who had made the Hajj pilgrimage to Mecca and then just tons of funky modern artwork and colors. As I stood staring, I heard a voice from inside: "*Tfaddal*" – come on in!

Meet Yasmin. Yasmin is a spunky, artistic Bedouin woman who lives in the village. As she was literally doing her laundry in front of me, she brought me water and candies and invited me to sit. We chatted and chatted. She works at a factory with Jews and she frankly liked to speak Hebrew with me while I spoke Arabic with her. To her, the North is a great place because "Jews and Arabs are brothers". She feels they work well together and have good relationships. Like most Israelis of all stripes, she is very, very fond of her hometown. She has relatives in nearby Arab villages, but she doesn't even like to visit there because home is where it's at. We talked about her mom who made the Hajj pilgrimage. Yasmin was very proud, but Yasmin herself didn't want to do it. She believes in God but not all the rituals and prayers—like not a small number of Jews.

Making my way down the hill to eat sushi with my kibbutznik friends who were hosting me (because yes, the Arab village has sushi), I couldn't help but think how hospitable a country this is. Both Jews and Arabs go out of their way to make you feel at home—with absolutely no expectation of something in return other than kindness and gratitude. Very, very few Americans would invite a stranger into their home like Yasmin or Eli did—even generous Americans. There is just a much greater sense of trust here and it's frankly refreshing. It even inspires me to be a more generous person.

Across the street from the sushi place, I saw a guy selling *nargeelah* (hookah). I popped into his store and good lord, if this was not one of the hottest people I've ever met, then slap me silly and call me a potato. His muscles were bulging. His face was gorgeous. And he had the friendliest smile to match. "I'll have what he's having."[33]

Murad is a 20-something Arab Greek Catholic man from a small village up north. He works in Tarshiha selling supplies for *nargeelah* at his own shop. As is the custom here, we talked all about life—where we're from, our background, our hopes and dreams. Because in Israel, you don't wait until five coffee dates in to get to know each other. He told me about his girlfriend—he said he feels no pressure from his family to get married or have children. That they're having a good time. And then it was my turn and I did something pretty brave and I came out to him. In Arabic. Alone. And…it was absolutely fine. I don't want to minimize the challenges of homophobia in any community, but since I got a positive vibe from him, I had a good feeling about it. He was very curious—he asked me how I knew, etc. etc.—the same kinds of questions I get even from liberal Americans.

When I explained that when people are attracted to the same sex, it's totally natural, and that you even find it in other species, he looked fascinated and frankly, just accepted it. No pushback, no antagonism, just kind of a "hmm never thought about it that way" look.

We exchanged contact info, gave a nice bro hug, and sent each other some pretty big smiles.

Until I did sushi that night, I had spent my entire day in Arabic other than a few Hebrew words sprinkled in. For all intents and purposes, I spent my day in the Arab world. And guess what? It was pretty cool. I met a Secular Greek Orthodox man, a Sunni Muslim Bedouin woman, and a (super-hot) Arab Greek Catholic guy with eye-popping muscles. I saw funky murals and artwork alongside ancient architecture. I even got delicious herbal melon tea at a cute cafe.

This is Arab Israel. Twenty percent of the country. If you haven't visited an Arab village do so. You don't really know Israel if you haven't. And if the extent of your visit is eating schwarma and going home—then you visited a restaurant, not a culture. Get off your tuchus[34], as we say in Yiddish, and try something new. Friends, food, and fun await you. *Tfaddal*—come on in! 😊

FRIENDSHIP

HOW ONE QUESTION CAN CHANGE YOUR LIFE

This story is unique to this collection and has never been featured on the blog.

I'VE LONG BEEN CURIOUS ABOUT BEDOUIN CULTURE. FROM THE TIME OF MY Birthright "Bedouin Tent Experience" at 18 to my Arabic courses in college, this subset of Arab culture has intrigued me.

Living in Tel Aviv, because of both distance and the way public transit is structured, it was much easier for me to explore Arab and Druze towns in the Center, Jerusalem, and the North.

For that very reason, I thought it was important to make an effort to get down south towards the desert. I had met some Bedouin up north (including the woman who fed me while she did her laundry in front of me, from an earlier story in this collection). But very few down south. Their environment, their climate, even their Arabic accents are different. And I wanted to see what it was all about. The best way to learn, as I discovered during my time in Israel, is by seeing for yourself.

After a day in Beersheva, I decided at night to go to Rahat, the largest Bedouin city in Israel. Apparently, they have authentic Bedouin food there, and I wanted to try a taste.

I got off my bus and I didn't know where to go. I was looking for a restaurant called "Mansaf", which is also a typical dish. It was dark out and I was definitely the only non-Bedouin hanging out in Rahat at night.

I saw a young man in front of me so I decided to approach him in Arabic: "Where is the Mansaf restaurant?" He pointed to his right and laughed—it was right next to me! How funny! This whole time, as I had gradually been getting nervous, it was standing right there.

Muhammad is a native of Rahat. At the time of this story he was 18 and was an avid fan of American cinema and TV. I later learned (because we decided to keep in touch) that he loved all sorts of TV I had never even heard of. Stuff with gore, with violence, with sex—things I didn't really expect from someone raised in such a conservative society. But according to Muhammad, his family was more chill. Just goes to show how far stereotypes can take you (hint: not very far).

Later on, I found myself helping Muhammad. He had decided to move to the Tel Aviv area to study accounting—a bold move for someone coming from what some might call the rural Oklahoma of Israel. Not because it's a bad place (I presume Oklahoma is all right too!), but because of the culture shock. Jewish and Arab societies rarely mix in Israel, even less so in the south.

So oddly enough, as a recently arrived immigrant to Israel, I found myself giving much the same advice I had received but to this wonderful Bedouin kid bravely moving away from home to pursue his dreams. A kind of *aliyah* advisor for Bedouin.

Muhammad and I have kept in touch for several years now, mostly via WhatsApp, although once I did come back down to visit him in the south.

I help him practice his English and answer his questions about American culture (no, we don't wear cowboy hats in Washington, D.C.). And he helps me practice my Arabic and keeps me up to date on the latest in Israeli and Arab culture.

It's a friendship that outlasted some of my American ones when I moved abroad. Sadly, some people really don't make the effort to keep in touch.

The good news is you can always make new friends. And when I first got on the plane to Israel, I never imagined that one of the kindest, warmest, and most open-minded of those would be someone named Muhammad.

That is the magic of one Arabic question asked on a summer night in the desert.

A GAY OL' TIME WATCHING ARABIC MASS
(I REALLY DON'T THINK THEY KNEW WE WERE GAY)

This story is unique to this collection and has never been featured on the blog.

ERIC IS AN AMERICAN CHRISTIAN. CATHOLIC TO BE PRECISE. AND IS REALLY cute. I met him because I sat at a cafe in East Jerusalem months before, spotted him sitting with a Swedish guy, and called over to say hello. I don't have one particular type, but if there was one, he was it.

Over the course of the next few weeks, we became fast friends, even if the differences between us were palpable. Political differences, age differences, life differences.

Eric liked guys. That part, among some other ones, did match up. And we kind of entered into a flirtation mixed with occasional conflict.

I told Eric it was important for him to see more of Israel, that it was just as good a place to practice his Arabic as the West Bank. He was studying in Hebron, perhaps the most tense place in the entire region.

We decided to go up north to my favorite part of Israel, and the most

49

heavily Arab. Things fluctuated between good and bad during the trip, though fortunately things ended well and we are friends to this day.

On the downside, there were moments where we kind of wanted to pull each other's hair out. And one of those moments was in Jish.

Jish is an Arab village in the Galilee. It's actually home to a few native Aramaic speakers and the Ministry of Education's Aramaic language program. Pretty cool.

I promised Eric some good churches. We went to the Maronite Church, which was pretty beautiful. The church interior was adorned with Aramaic artwork and calligraphy. I'm glad we could get in.

Then we were looking for the other Catholic church—it may have been Greek Catholic, I can't recall. There are more denominations of Christianity in the Middle East than you could possibly imagine. Although America does a good job of that, too.

I knocked on door after door in the neighborhood around the church to try to find the key to get in. I could tell Eric was kind of bored and I wanted to show off how cool the Galilee was to him. And to help diffuse some of the tension the trip had caused.

I finally came across someone who answered their door. Maryam, a woman from the village, said the key wasn't available right now because the person who held it was out of town.

But being the gentle and hospitable soul that she was, she immediately invited us in.

One thing I've learned from speaking Arabic is that this is not a suggestion, it's kind of a heartfelt command.

We came in, me and my semi-lover, and watched two hours of Lebanese Catholic mass beamed via satellite from our northern neighbors. As much as I love mass (I actually have been to a number of them in Arabic and it's really cool), I'm glad the TV stream was punctuated by conversation with Maryam and her family. And lots of cookies and tea.

As we left, I couldn't help but think how Arabic had brought this all together. Eric was studying the language, bringing him to the region. I spoke it, which built a pretty strong connection to Eric and Maryam. And it's the reason we had come to the village and the north in the first place. It's why we ended up in this woman's living room watching Lebanese mass on TV.

Arabic is a magical language. As all languages have the capacity to be.

But good thing for Eric and me we also have English—there was enough lost in translation in our native tongue!

A JEW, TWO DRUZE, AND A CHRISTIAN WALK ONTO A TRAIN...

Nope, not a joke, just a regular afternoon 😊

PlantingRootsBearingFruits.com, May 21, 2018

TODAY WAS TIRING, SO I THOUGHT IT'D BE NICE TO REMEMBER A REALLY hopeful story from my travels in Israel.

I had gone up to Haifa to explore and was taking the train back to Tel Aviv. The train in Israel is not just a vehicle—it's the town square. People chat, gossip, exchange numbers—even make friends. It's a place that reflects the warmth of this country more than any other place on the planet I've visited. You're never really alone on the train. Sometimes that means loud music and conversations, but it's never boring and it just feels like home.

There was one seat left in a four-seat area. Three 20-something guys were talking in Arabic.

I sat down, and after about a minute I chimed in in Arabic. They were stunned. I love sharing how I speak Arabic with Arabs here. I recently made a video in Arabic[35] about how and why I learned the language. In short, I learned Syrian Arabic with a professor from Damascus in America and then with Syrian refugees on Skype. Which you can do, too[36]. For an Arab here to hear an American-Israeli Jew speaking Syrian Arabic is a bit like an American hearing a North Korean speaking like a native New Yorker. People are often in amazement. It's great. 😊 I like melting hearts.

One guy was a Christian from Mi'ilya, one of my favorite villages in Israel. It's a Greek Catholic Arab village that I've visited twice. They have a beautiful historic church and it's near a Crusader castle I want to visit. The people are so warm. They even have a cool locally-made chocolate shop! For the linguistically inclined among us, they also speak with a "qaf" or what we write in English as a "q"- usually a trait of Druze villages here. It was really cool to find that out.

And to find out that one of the Druze guys comes from Yarka, a village that despite being Druze, actually doesn't use the "qaf" but instead uses a hamza, or "hiccup" sound. So for instance, the word "qalb" or "heart" in Arabic would be pronounced *'alb*. In short, the Christian speaks like the Druze and the Druze like the Christian—at least on this train. 😊

Except for the super-hot Druze guy next to me. See, the Christian and the Druze guys across from me were in school together in the south of Israel. It can be hard to tell with Arab men because they have very intimate male friendships, but I actually kind of wondered if they were a couple. They'd make a cute one. 😊 I noticed a lot of physical and emotional closeness. It was sweet either way.

Back to the hot Druze guy. 😊 He uses the "qaf" like most Druze. He wasn't in school, he was in the army. He had a gorgeous, warm, inviting smile. A beautiful laugh. A kind heart. And an outside just as beautiful.

We talked a lot. All of us. Turns out each village even has its own *kubbeh*, a Middle Eastern food usually involving meat stuffed into a kind of fried covering. What I didn't know is that there are villages up north with RAW kubbeh. Yes, the kubbeh meat isn't cooked! I joked with them that if they opened a restaurant in Tel Aviv and called it Arab Sushi, they'd make a million bucks. We laughed. 😊

When they got off the train, I was sad to see them go. I gave the Druze soldier my number and told him and his friends to be in touch when they come to Tel Aviv.

Then, the most curious and beautiful thing happened.

Two Sephardic Haredi[37] men—also pretty young—moved over to my section. They study in Yeshiva, seminary, in Ofakim. They needed help figuring out possible routes home, so I opened my app. They don't have smartphones—a lot of ultra-Orthodox don't. In order to keep out unwanted Internet content, etc. They were really nice and I helped them find some ways home.

Both of them are of Moroccan origin. We talked about their yeshiva—I was familiar with Shas[38] yeshivas in that they tend to be modeled after Lithuanian ones. The ones my ancestors prayed in. 😊 We talked about Sephardic culture—they didn't know about Ladino! Ladino[39] was less of a Moroccan thing (although they had a dialect called Haketia which was similar), but they were astounded to learn about this Judeo-Spanish language! And they're going to search for Ladino music at home…because I think they have YouTube there. I didn't ask. 😊

Then the best question came up: "So, what were you talking with those kids about in Arabic?" I smiled. But before I could answer, they said: "We think you were talking about food!"

And they were right! I told them all about our conversation. Their eyes lit up. They were eager and willing to learn about all that we discussed. And in a spirit of curiosity. About their neighbors.

As I left the train, I couldn't help but feel satisfied. I was the bridge between two Druze, a Christian, and two ultra-Orthodox Sephardic Jews. When people ask me what I do with my eight languages (expecting that I work for the military or make loads of money)—this is what I do. If people want to work in other fields, that's great. We need multilingual people in intelligence. The intelligence I'm doing is on how to bring people together. I use my Hebrew, my Arabic, and other languages to live a happy, healthy, and fulfilling life. That hopefully shares some of that joy with others.

I couldn't have had this experience without speaking both Hebrew and Arabic. One thing I've realized lately is that I can't translate some of my feelings to English. I'm thoroughly Israeli. I think and feel in Hebrew—and in Arabic. Often better than in English. This is where my soul breathes and lives to the fullest. America feels cold to me—distant, polite, dull, preoccupied with the self.

Israel is a place of great warmth. Among every sector of society. It's astounding and a beautiful thing to be a part of. I'm grateful for the dozens of people who host me for meals and to stay in their homes. I pass that warmth on to the people around me. Like when I met a lone soldier on the bus the other day from New Jersey, far from home on his birthday. And took him out to baklava and Eritrean food and hosted him for the night.

Find me an American—in America—who does that. It just doesn't happen. I'm sure there are sociological reasons, fear, crime, who knows. There
are reasons for everything, sometimes valid and sometimes that don't match
up with the facts.

All I know is that in Israel, we are direct[40], we are generous, we are
honest. I never have to guess what an Israeli is thinking. Even if I don't like
what they say—I know they'll speak their mind. And I can say I don't like it
either. We can be truthful.

And the honest truth is this: At a time when America is crumbling—when Republicans and Democrats struggle to even be friends. When my liberal friends bash evangelicals. And right-wingers pretend anything that doesn't fit with their worldview is "fake news"…

In Israel, we have a glue that keeps us together. Perhaps out of necessity, but also just because this is a special place with special people. Who tend to have a real depth of kindness and a zest for life.

You might like to hate on us for what's going on in Gaza or barely utter a peep when Iran launches missiles at the Golan. But in the end, for all the conflict here, Israelis—we're a hell of a lot better than Americans (or Europeans) at actually getting along.

That's a sentence that might be hard to stomach—or maybe to believe. If that's the case, you're probably not Israeli. 😊 It's true—there's a lot of beef between all the sectors of society I spoke to on that train. But you know what? You're never going to see my interaction on CNN. Because they've decided that only dead bodies are sexy.

But guess what? So are Druze soldiers talking, smiling at an American-Israeli whose life is now a whole lot more hummus than grilled cheese.

P.S. That photo is the Druze flag with a Magen David, the Star of David. Because I love Druze. 😊

WHAT'S BEYOND
THE HUMMUS STAND?

PlantingRootsBearingFruits.com, June 6, 2018

TODAY, I WAS SUPPOSED TO GO TO HACARMEL PARK FOR A HIKE TO A DRUZE village.

The bus ended up taking forever so I decided to hop off and explore another adventure.

For a while, I've been Fureidis[41]-curious. The Arab village, decidedly not on any tourist map, is just north of Zichron Yaakov, one of my favorite scenic spots in Israel.

I've frequently gazed at Fureidis from Zichron, at its beautiful gold-topped mosque, and wondered what was there. After some very close calls in Muslim Arab villages, I have been hesitant to visit them alone. While some places like Abu Ghosh are always safe, some of my more adventurous trips to Kafr Qasem and Tira involved some scary situations. Most people were awesome and I had a great time. And for a few moments, I did worry about my safety.

Today, I felt the spirit was with me and decided to march up the hill. Fureidis starts at sea level and goes all the way up a mountain. It's stunning.

This being a small village, especially from a segment of society where there's a lack of trust of the government, people coming from the outside, and sometimes Jews—I knew what I had to do. The first four or five people I talked to, I introduced myself, explained who I was, where I was from, and how I learned Arabic (important, because I speak Syrian which sounds out of the ordinary here). As is the case in many villages, I had to explain why I wanted to take pictures and, in short, earn people's trust.

In order to get into the mosque, I spoke with one man to get directions. I bumped into him— perhaps not coincidentally, up by the mosque again, but this time on a tractor. Samir was very friendly and took a picture of me smiling. I would not be surprised if I'm in some village WhatsApp group now. I understand what it means to build trust, so I welcomed it. Samir then told me he had called a man who could let me into the mosque.

While I was allowed to take pictures outside, pictures inside were not allowed. This was the first time this had happened in Israel, and I wondered why. I've even filmed prayers in many mosques. Perhaps there is a dispute about land usage, building rights, who knows. Maybe it's just suspicion of an outsider—because it's readily apparent that so few Jews (or non-Muslims) visit here.

It was a very welcoming conversation—Muhammad, the other man, was a really warm person. And as he saw my intentions were good, he opened up. And we talked about Ramadan prayers, the history of the building, the delicious *qamar al-din* [42] drink (which I didn't realize was made from apricots!), and his own wild adventures in the nearby forest as a youth.

I then headed to the forest. Every step of the way, I asked people for directions, even when I knew more or less where I was going. This makes me known and builds trust. Remember that the police, even Arab police, work throughout Israel, and don't always have strong relationships with the local

populace. I was once told by a Druze boy—the Druze are solidly Zionist—
that some people would be suspicious of me in the village. Not because I was
Jewish, but because they thought I was a cop. Even an undercover Druze
cop.

I walked through the forest, which was amazing. The trees stood still,
the air was clear, the ground rough and clay-like in color. Except when radi-
ant bits of cream-colored stone poked through.

It was like a Middle Eastern fairy tale.

To my right, I noticed some sheep. How cool! How many places in
the world can you take a single bus line from a metropolis and end up on a
mountaintop with sheep?!

Next to the adorable sheep was some sort of structure. It looked vaguely
like a trailer, an RV. I suppose it was a house. Perhaps one built without
legal permission—I have no clue. I do know that it's a hot political issue, so

I didn't take any pictures. I didn't want people to think I was there to report them or cause trouble.

Two adorable kids, one nine and one 15, came running over to me. "Who are you?" I told them I was from Tel Aviv (and America and was Jewish) and had studied Arabic in college. I asked what they were doing. They said they were picking vegetables. There was a large garden, one might even say small farm, all around the house.

Without asking, they start handing me cucumbers. Fresh, delicious, crisp cucumbers. Straight from the garden. Unwashed and unbeatable.

While I chowed down, we chatted. One of the kids is a Barça fan. He had a Messi shirt on and I told him it's my team too. 😊 And that I visited there! He was amazed. Too bad the other kid liked Real Madrid; we made fun of him. 😊

It's hard to describe to someone who doesn't speak Arabic, but Arab kids here have a certain sweetness to them. When I talk with them in Arabic, there's a warmth—and it doesn't matter if they're Druze, Christian, or Muslim. There's a playfulness, a sense of fun, and kindhearted sincerity with laughter. In a country where things can get rough around the edges, I find myself living in a deep, deep smile when I talk to Arab young people.

Their father came over and we talked in a mixture of Hebrew and Arabic about his farm. All of the food is for his family. He has five children. And they live in the middle of the woods—it sounded absolutely fantastic. Maybe I'll do it one day. All of his vegetables are organic and he has no desire to sell them—they simply feed his family. Like I suppose all of us did back in the day.

Suddenly another son appeared with an injured lip. I asked what happened. Apparently, their horses—because yes, they have horses—hurt him. And he giggled. While bringing me half a dozen more cucumbers. Mmmmm.

We talked briefly about the lack of summer opportunities for kids (they mostly work) and how expensive schooling is (in Israel you have to pay for public school), but honestly I was more worked up about it than he was. *"Mah laasot?"*—what can you do? That was his response. It was pretty clear to me he was more focused on living and not really interested in politics or complaining. Just recognizing challenges and moving on to get the most out of things.

As I headed down the hill, I couldn't help but think how important it was to share this story.

Personally, I've experienced this dozens of times in Israel. Being invited into Bedouin, Druze, Christian—all sorts of Arabic-speaking homes. Sitting sometimes for hours with people I had never met and had never made plans with. Just enjoying and talking and being with each other.

Very, very few Israeli Jews (or foreigners who come to visit—even to protest against my country) have had this experience. And I'd like them to be able to enjoy it.

Because it is only with the power of language—and certainly a heavy dose of self-awareness and trust-building—that this happens. This doesn't happen because you read Ari Shavit or because you went to a political rally or because you ate hummus at an Arab diner or because you boycott Israel (good luck with that—this Arab town is in our country and the man who gave me a tour of the mosque used the phrase "Israeli Arabs" in Arabic). Or any other of the multitude of superficial ways to engage with Arab culture, even when well-intentioned.

At a time when my country is under vicious attack by Hamas extremists, setting fire to thousands of acres[43] of land and firing hundreds of rockets at my friends in the South, I built trust and had fun. It was good for my heart, good for the people I befriended, and good for my country. And I felt great.

To bring a little hope into the world, I speak Arabic. I speak it because it's beautiful, it's related to Hebrew, it's fun to mix them, it opens hearts, it feels special to me.

I speak it so my nine-year old friend will grow up one day and remember, despite all the political tension, that a nice Jewish guy came around and joked with him about soccer teams in Arabic. The only language he speaks. That we, that I, care. And maybe that will help bring a little more love and less conflict into the world.

It's my firm belief that to learn a language you must fall in love with it. Its sounds, its melody, its letters, its culture, its food, its history, its culture, its geography. The grammar, the art, the calligraphy. So that every chance you get to speak it, you do! Not because you have to—this is the worst reason to learn a language. But rather, because you want to. You enjoy it, it brings you to a state of mind where you're feeling good and passing that on to the interesting people you're meeting. Face to face, heart to heart.

None of my day would've been possible without Arabic. If you had gone to the same village only knowing English or Hebrew (or for that matter, Arabic without Hebrew—our Arabic here is sprinkled with it), you would've gotten as far as the hummus stand. It just doesn't build love here in the same way, to the same degree.

You want in on the fun? To explore the real depth of this country, places few of your friends have even visited but are begging you to enjoy?

Here's a unique opportunity. I'm going to open an Adventure Arabic class. We'll learn together with the goal of going on a *tiyyul*, or trip, together at the end of the course. To an Arabic-speaking village. So that your Arabic won't sit at home rusting, but you'll rather get the chance to speak it in real life.

Because of the unique nature of Israeli Arabic, you need to already have a fairly strong command of Hebrew. And besides that, a desire to learn and discover.

Come see what's beyond the hummus stand 😊

AN AMAZING DAY THAT CAN
ONLY HAPPEN HERE

PlantingRootsBearingFruits.com, March 1, 2018

TODAY, I HAD THE MOST FASCINATING AND FABULOUS DAY.

I started the morning in Shefa'mr[44] (Shefaram) in Hebrew. Shefa'mr is the most pluralistic city in Israel. A community with Druze, Muslims, and Christians, it is one of the rare places in Israel where people of different faiths live next door to each other. As a matter of practice. Not like Jerusalem, where there are different groups largely in different neighborhoods. Literally side by side.

It's one of the reasons I wanted to visit. The other reason is it, like the North, is absolutely gorgeous. Take a look at some of my pictures:

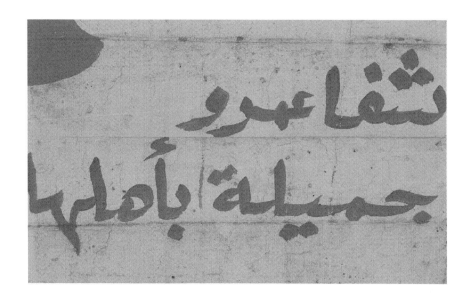

hummus and pita and falafel from a Druze restaurant. According to the owner, apparently the town loves Argentina's soccer team. Someone even went to the World Cup in Brazil to cheer them on. You'll see from the pictures below that I took today that he's telling the truth, although you'll also see there seems to be a (rival?) Brazilian fan club:

Not what I expected to find when I came to live in the Middle East. Which makes it all the more interesting and fun to discover! I love finding things that challenge my assumptions.

In the village, I visited churches, mosques, and a Druze holy site. There's even a synagogue. There's even an ice cream shop that sells KNAFE ICE CREAM! If you don't know what knafe is, it's this[45]. And it's delicious, even as ice cream.

I was the only tourist in town today. Not sure how many come on other days, but I definitely didn't meet another outsider—not even another Israeli Jew. And by and large, people were really nice. It's important to remember there are toxic and kind people everywhere (and a whole lot of people somewhere in between). I've learned that people of all backgrounds live in gray space and nuance—it has frankly allowed me to see Arabs as people. Rather than exoticizing them as all good or all bad or "Christian ones are good and Muslims are bad" (as many, many Israeli Jews say)—I've worked really hard to get to the point where I just see them as people. Complex, like me. It has added a softness to my Arabic that makes the language gentler and even more fun to speak.

I met with all sorts of fascinating people today—the Muslim woman who keeps the keys to the synagogue, the zany ice cream store owner who couldn't believe a Jew could speak Arabic like me, the Druze women who wanted me to explain Donald Trump to them.

There's a gentleness to Shefa'mr. It's kind of a preview of how this place could look with more peace and harmony. More mixing and less hatred. Or perhaps a view into a past here that once was. Like my photo of a Greek Catholic Cross in front of the mosque, Shefa'mr is about living together. In the words of a Druze woman: "One of our neighbors is Christian, the other Muslim. Yes, there is racism, like anywhere else. But we share in our sorrows and we share in our joys together."

Before I visited Shefa'mr, when I was deciding whether to go, a Jewish Israeli asked me: "Why would you go there? What is there to see?" When you meet someone like this, ignore them. She's missing out and it's truly sad to live in such ignorance of the beauty at your doorstep. Shefa'mr is gorgeous and I did some amazing peaceful thinking there today.

After a thoughtful and inspirational morning in Shefa'mr, I hopped on a bus and then a train back to Tel Aviv. I hate coming back home to Tel Aviv these days. The city is loud, the people are often rude; there is an intensity to life here that just sucks sometimes.

Luckily, a friend had invited me out for Purim[46], today's Jewish holiday. In the U.S., we tend to eat hamantaschen[47], read the megillah, have carnivals for kids, dress up in costumes, and if you're a young professional, maybe go to a party. It's fun and it's decidedly low-key compared to what I experienced today.

Tel Aviv Purim is Jewish Mardi Gras. It's Carnaval. It's Jewish Sao Paolo going nuts—and it's amazing. I don't drink. I do dance. I do love to talk to random people, including shirtless Jewish boys who are feeling friendly. Purim is party after party—in the street, in the club. Everyone is happy. I have never, ever seen so many Israeli Jews smile and laugh at once. And it goes on for several days—today was just day one.

I've never been to a cooler Jewish party in my life. It's huge. And fun. And for this one moment in time, Israeli Jews let go of the stress and basically don't give a f*ck. They just relax and have fun.

I had such a great time. I suppose the intensity that I hate in Tel Aviv has its occasional advantages. I can't imagine a small town in Israel—Jewish or otherwise—putting together this level of festivity. It's amazing.

I haven't yet experienced all the holidays in Israel. I have experienced most of them. Purim is now my favorite Israeli holiday. It's like New Orleans filled with cute Jewish boys, dance music, and silly (sometimes racist) costumes.

If I had it my way, every month, maybe even every week would be Purim. Israeli Jews need release. And perhaps if they had more of it, more of them would be more relaxed.

My day started with Druze, Christians, and Muslims and ended with a street fair in Tel Aviv. Few people here live like I do. And I encourage more to do so in the way that they can. Cross boundaries. Speak Arabic in the morning in the hillsides and rock out to Britney Spears at night. Discover the secret Argentinean fan club in an Arab village and then flirt with half naked men in Hebrew as the sun rises.

I'm happy I found my way today. My way to a good day, a fantastic day. A day that even ended with flirting with a non-Jewish German I met while walking home to my apartment—he's a nurse at the hospital around the corner!

This place where I live is both terrible and full of magic. As I drift to sleep after an incredible day, I'm glad I lived today the way I did.

May it inspire us to find the stars shining where we least expect them.

DRUZE MAKE THE BEST ZIONISTS
(AND KUBBEH)

PlantingRootsBearingFruits.com, August 17, 2017

WHO ARE THE DRUZE? THE DRUZE[48] ARE AN ARABIC-SPEAKING MINORITY IN Israel, Lebanon, Syria, and Jordan. They have their own secret monotheistic religion that was often persecuted by Muslim rulers.

By their creed, they are loyal to the state they live in. Druze serve in the Lebanese, Syrian, Jordanian, and Israeli armies. In Israel, they voluntarily signed a pact with the state for their sons to be drafted into the army. Other Arabic-speakers are not legally obligated (some choose to volunteer). It's important to note that in Israel, many Druze simply identify as Druze and not as Arabs due to their Zionism, their previous persecution by Muslims, and societal pressure to distinguish themselves from the Arab minority.

Today I went to Daliat al-Karmel[49], a Druze village, to see what they're all about. First off, this place is gorgeous:

I started off the day by buying local Druze music. Or as I like to call it, Druzic. (The puns are innumerable—just think, if Druze drank, you could have a "Druze booze cruise"!) At this little hole-in-the-wall shop, I got three CDs by local singers in Arabic—two pop CDs and one of wedding/folk music. I can't wait to pop them in my iPod. If your only experience in a Druze village is eating hummus, you are an awful tourist. Go try something new that expands your cultural boundaries.

I did go eat amazing Druze food, including the best kubbeh[50] I've ever had. For my American friends who've traveled in the South—it somehow tasted like hush puppies[51] but better. My waiter was an 18-year-old man who was very excited to hear me speaking Arabic and also told me all about how he was going into the army in December.

Then I wandered around and ended up at a Druze holy site: the cave of the Prophet Abu Ibrahim[52]. The Druze visitors kiss the doorway as they enter, much like Jews kiss mezuzahs[53]. Everyone must take off their shoes and wear long sleeves, including men (some women put a long-sleeved shirt on me). I wandered into this stone cave where there were candles. I was all alone, so I spoke out loud to God. We had a good conversation. It was one of the most spiritual moments I've ever had. Me and God alone in a cave in a Druze village.

Then I came out and went to a memorial for Druze soldiers who were killed while serving in the IDF[54]. I was so moved. These are non-Jews whose community chose to put their lives on the line to protect my right as a Jew to live here and their right to live in peace. Eighty percent of Druze men serve in the Israeli military, a higher percentage than Jews. As I stood at the wall of names, I said Kaddish[55] out loud for these brave men as the breeze swooshed by and you could almost hear their souls rustling in the trees. Another powerful spiritual experience.

The memorial is a reminder that not all Jews are Zionists and not all Zionists are Jews. I've met a number of Jewish anti/non-Zionists in Tel Aviv. Some are disaffected Israelis born here who are looking for a better life in another country or have political qualms. I can understand that to an extent, even if I disagree—this place can be difficult economically and there are real religious and political issues here. Other anti-Zionists here are *olim* (new immigrants). Now this frustrates the hell out of me. You want to take advantage of the fact that you're Jewish to receive money from the state, citizenship, and a free flight. Then, you want to go around telling everyone how you're not a Zionist? You might not be a Zionist, but you are a hypocrite. Criticizing Israel out of the spirit of bettering the country is democracy. Demonizing us is not. Our people didn't die for you to have the opportunity to enjoy the privileges of being Israeli only to use that privilege to trash us. Against Zionism? Then don't come to Zion. There are plenty of English teaching jobs in Korea.

Meanwhile, non-Jews like Druze put their lives on the line for us to survive. And at great cost. There are even some Druze who are pushing back against military service because of the tensions it creates with their Arab neighbors and because of poorly-funded municipalities. All Jews should become "Jews for Druze" (I've loved that name for years) and help our brethren feel appreciated for their sacrifices.

Before I headed off, I stopped into a store for some water. As often happens with me here in Israel, this became a three-hour Arabic and Hebrew discussion with a local Druze family. Samir's family runs the store. In his own words, he is a secular Druze (something I've never heard of but piqued my curiosity). His wife is a devout Druze woman. According to Samir, this is legitimate in their community, but if it were the other way around, it'd be perceived as problematic. He said this was very much "inside baseball" and I loved the insight he was sharing. All his children are secular Druze and are doing some combination of army and school. His daughter is studying to be an engineer.

I explained to him I was a Reform Jew (which surprisingly he understood—more than some Jews here I've met!). As we were talking about spirituality and identity, I actually did something very brave and came out to him as gay. In the middle of a rural Druze village. I was nervous about his response, but to be honest, he barely made note of it. We just continued our great conversation as his wife plied me with walnut-stuffed dates. We even exchanged numbers and he said he'd invite me to a local wedding sometime. Interesting things do happen here!

In short, we're taught in the U.S. not to generalize about people. And usually I agree. But in this case, I'll make an exception: Druze are awesome. I love them. They are righteous gentiles who support my people and my right to live in my homeland. And they make delicious food. I will support them as well. They've earned it. If you're Israeli or Jewish or just a good person, support this fascinating minority. We should never take such friends for granted.

BEDOUIN ARABIC . . .
IN HASIDIC BNEI BRAK

PlantingRootsBearingFruits.com, April 10, 2018

Yes, the title is exactly what you think.

As an appropriate sequel to my blog "Bedouin Yiddish[56]", in which I discovered a Bedouin man who speaks Yiddish in Rahat, I found Bedouin speaking Arabic in Bnei Brak!

Before we get to that, let's start at the very beginning[57].

Today, I was planning on visiting the West Bank. Area C, where Israelis can visit, is where I've made contact with a Palestinian practitioner of non-violence who partners with Israelis (including settlers). However, feeling rattled after yesterday's "preview of a terrorist attack[58]", I decided I wasn't in the right frame of mind to make the most out of the experience.

Instead, I made my way to Bnei Brak[59]. I've written a lot about this Haredi city of 200,000 people on the doorstep of Tel Aviv. My first Haredi

hug[60], my first time praying in a Hasidic shtiebl[61], Satmar Yiddish newspa-
pers[62], the hot guys[63], and the time I got a blessing[64] from a Vizhnitz Hasid.

Speaking of Vizhnitz, that's exactly where I went today. Kiryat Vizhnitz,
named after the town in Europe where the Hasidic dynasty[65] was founded, is
a part of Bnei Brak I knew less about.

Knowing that there was a renowned Vizhnitz bakery AND a Yemenite
Haredi bookstore, I knew this was my destination for the day. Quench the
thirst of my soul and my stomach!

I started at Nosach Teiman[66], a Yemenite Jewish[67] bookstore and
Judaica shop. The riches of this small store are innumerable. I bought loads
of Yemenite music, a Judeo-Ara*maic* calendar (!!), prayers written in Judeo-
Arabic, and a book of Judeo-Arabic expressions translated into Hebrew. It
does not get any better than this. Here are some pics:

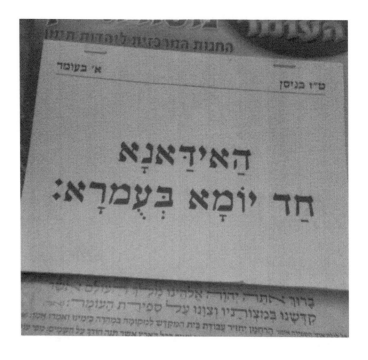

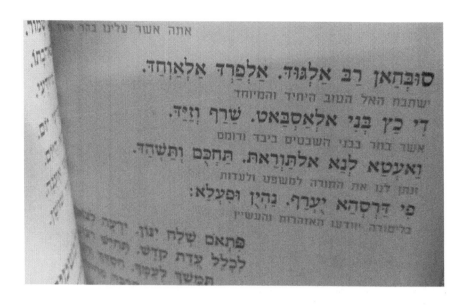

They even had Yemenite Jewish clothing, make-up, and perfume for sale. For a community that had to escape by the skin of its teeth from fanatical neighbors who wanted to exterminate them, they've sure done an amazing job of preserving their culture upon arriving to Israel. While unfortunately fewer and fewer Yemenites here speak their unique language, I did hear a few words in the store which I could mostly understand with my Arabic!

Energized, I headed to the Vizhnitz bakery, sure that I'd also find new adventures on the way. On my way there, I came across several yeshivas. The first, a Sephardic one, where I got a free book called "Mishnah Brurah". It's old and beautiful—and free. Bnei Brak is one of the few places on the planet where you'll find timeless beautiful books simply sitting outside waiting for you to grab them. For free or minimal cost. These are the Jews who truly continue to embody that we are the "People of the Book". Looking for Jewish knowledge? Skip Amazon and head to shuls in Bnei Brak.

Down the street, I saw the Belz[68] Yeshiva. There's a famous song[69] about the shtetl, or Jewish village, of Belz that once existed in Eastern Europe. So, to see the town recreated in front of my eyes—its Jewish presence in Europe exterminated—was awe-inspiring. As Holocaust Remembrance Day approaches in Israel, I couldn't help but let out a huge smile. As the famous Yiddish resistance song[70] says: Mir zaynen do. We are here. In the face of Nazi persecution[71], Christian annihilation[72], Islamic fundamentalism[73], ever-shifting anti-Semitism on both left and right- we exist. We survived. We. are. here.

To see my heritage continue in the face of 2,000 years of European brutality[74] is a miracle. It fills me with hope, wonder, amazement, and joy. Our mere presence is a victory in and of itself.

I headed to the bakery with a fulfilled soul and a hungry stomach.

The bakery was delicious. It was nothing but challahs left and right. Some huge, some small and all a bit sweet.

While I noshed on my challah, I noticed something interesting—a sign with baking instructions in Arabic. Bnei Brak is 1000% Jewish. A mixed city this is not. A secular person moving here would be considered a mixed population.

Then I noticed a tan-skinned man yelling in Hebrew at a Hasid. Something about business. Given how everyone yells in my neighborhood— even when not angry—I didn't make much of it. Must just be a Mizrachi[75] guy who does business with Vizhnitz bakers.

Then I heard the most unexpected thing ever: Arabic. And not Yemenite Judeo-Arabic. Arabic from here. I approached the tan men in Arabic. Their eyes widened with excitement and surprise. You have to remember I'm wearing a black yarmulke, a kippa, a head covering. I look, for all intents and purposes, Modern Orthodox[76].

Turns out, they're Bedouins. I told them I had been to Rahat (where I discovered the Yiddish speaker). They said they lived in a nearby town of Ad-Dhahiriya[77], whose name at first I confused with Nahariya, a city in the North of Israel. Only once I googled its name did I realize…it's a Palestinian city. In the West Bank.

We had a great talk about the Bedouin *dahiyye* music I like (they're going to teach me the dance next time) and I was proud to hear, as I walked away, them say *"wallahi byehki arabi mneeh"*. Wow, he really speaks Arabic well. My smile inside and out could not be bigger even as I write this now.

While Yemenite Arabic in Israel is struggling, I found Bedouin Palestinians who are keeping Arabic alive in Bnei Brak. While my trip to the West Bank didn't happen today, I did end up meeting Palestinians. And having fun. And hopefully warming a few hearts, like they did mine.

Still hungry, I grabbed a sweet for the road. The man at the store turned out to be a fellow polyglot. He spoke Hebrew, Yiddish, French, and English. And a straight-up Haredi Jew. We shared a fantastic short conversation in all languages. I bet you didn't expect that in Bnei Brak. Or the gluten-free falafel I found. Or the multilingual dictionaries for learning Arabic, Hindi, Chinese, Italian, Spanish, Farsi, and Yiddish (the latter possibly for Mizrachi Jews). All alongside a sign for "kosher" phones that filter out "non-kosher" content.

What I hope you take from this adventure is the unexpected mystery and glory of finding new places and new people. Bnei Brak is an awe-inspiring place. With things that will surprise you if you open your mind and heart to the possibilities.

On my way back to Tel Aviv for a Eurovision concert headlined by Dana International, Israel's first transgender superstar, I felt sad taking my yarmulke off. I like my black yarmulke. It suits me. Not as a decoration and not just as a sign of respect for Bnei Brak. But because I like that part of me. That heimish, passionately Jewish, bookish, dancing-down-the-aisles Matt. The Hasidic part of me. The Haredi part of me.

And I don't like feeling that I need to take it off when I come back to Tel Aviv, especially at an event with a lot of gay people. Who—and I understand why—would be afraid to talk to me because of it.

This is what I hope we can one day overcome—on all sides. I long for the day when I can be a gay Hasidic Jew, with the flexibility to still pray Reform and to go to gay parties. And find a gay partner. I long for the day when secular gay people will accept my passion for Judaism, including Orthodox Judaism, as a part of me.

I shouldn't have to sacrifice bits of my soul to keep other people happy. Nobody fits into a box— boxes are boring. I'm glad I explore different things and my life is much, much richer for it, even with the challenges.

When I go to Bnei Brak now, I'm not just a visitor. I know this place. And I like some of it. I hope it continues to passionately preserve its Judaism and I hope it can find ways to be more inclusive of people like me. And I don't know how possible it is to do both. I would like to try—I suppose I already am.

So next gay party, don't be surprised if I put on my yarmulke for a bit— just to see how it feels. And to see how you react.

And next visit to Bnei Brak, don't be surprised if I linger a bit under your city's rainbow-colored flag to take a selfie. Because inside it feels really queer.

Just like speaking Bedouin Arabic in the middle of a Hasidic bakery.

BE A GOOD ISRAELI
AND LEARN ARABIC

PlantingRootsBearingFruits.com, November 13, 2017

TODAY I HAD SOME PHENOMENAL EXPERIENCES IN ISRAEL—ONLY BECAUSE I speak Arabic. Rather than write a post with facts and figures about why my fellow Israelis should learn the language, I'm going to simply share my story.

This afternoon, I stopped by a sandwich shop. While the chef made me a chicken in pita sandwich, I asked him where in the neighborhood I could buy a notebook. He said he was new to the area so he didn't know. I told him I was new, too. He lives in North Tel Aviv but happens to work at this restaurant a couple days a week, only as of recently.

After explaining I was an *oleh chadash*, a newly-minted Israeli, he welcomed me and asked where I was from. I then asked him what his family's origin was. Turns out he's Moroccan and moved to Israel when he was very young. Not looking more than 35 years old, I was stunned. Most Moroccan

Jews in Israel moved during the 1950s. He even grew up speaking Moroccan at home—something rare among young Israelis. We switched to Arabic. I told him how cool it was to talk to a Jew in Arabic. In America, where 90% of Jews are Ashkenazi, it's almost unthinkable to find a native Arabic speaker in your synagogue. And yet here I was talking with a 35-year-old Moroccan Jew in Arabic.

Wrong. Amir (pseudonym) is Moroccan but, to the surprise of probably everyone reading this, is Muslim. And not a convert—a Muslim by birth.

How did we get here? So first off, Amir tells me he grew up in Tira. I've heard of Tira before and I did some googling to double check—yes, in fact, it is an Arab town. It'd be quite out of the ordinary to find Moroccan Jews living in the middle of an Arab village here. In addition, while many Moroccans can get by in Levantine Arabic[78] (the dialect I speak along with Arab-Israelis/Palestinians), he had a strong facility with the language and didn't revert to any Moroccan-isms. I'm familiar with some because several of my college Arabic professors were Moroccan.

So finally I asked him: "Tira is an Arab village—are you Jewish?" I figured maybe, working in the neighborhood we were in, he might be afraid to reveal his identity. He then told me he wasn't Jewish but was most certainly Moroccan. So then the obvious question—how on earth did he get here? For those of you unfamiliar, Israel and Morocco don't even have mutual embassies, let alone coordinated immigration policies.

At this point, there's a Jewish Israeli sitting in the cafe, too. Moshe is of Moroccan descent, but barely speaks the language. But of course, even though Amir had told me over and over how great my Arabic was, this other shmo had to tell me I don't speak like an Arab—which is bullshit because I have a great accent. Like most insecure people, he chose to take his own identity issues out on me (look for a future blog on Mizrachi identity).

Noticing the other patron, Amir turns away from him and leans in to tell me: "It's a secret, but my family worked with the Israeli government and that's why we were able to come."

Wow. First of all, I have absolutely no way to verify it. But in the interest of protecting his privacy, I did use a pseudonym and will not reveal the restaurant. I do have to say though that after having talked for about an hour, he seemed like a legit guy and I don't have any reason to question what he said.

As I headed out from the restaurant, we gave each other a smile and a hearty "*ma asalaameh*". Nice to make a new friend!

Still in shock and full of adrenaline, I walked through Tel Aviv until I found myself hungry again. This time, I popped into a Cofix, a cafe here, and no joke, I heard my favorite Egyptian pop song. It's something that's literally on my phone right now.

Seeing as how almost no Arabs live in the center of Tel Aviv, I was pleasantly surprised. I went in and addressed the young man in Arabic: "Hey, is this your music?" He looked a bit confused. So I switched to Hebrew. And it turns out, yes this is his music.

I switched back to Arabic but found he only understood about half of what I was saying. And not because, like Moshe thought, I "can't speak like an Arab". Rather, it's because he's not Arab—he's Jewish!

What?!? Okay so this kid, Nir, his family is Syrian. His parents speak Syrian Arabic at home—the exact dialect I speak. He grew up with it and in his own words "is in love with Arabic". Which is why he blares the music in his cafe in the middle of Tel Aviv.

I asked him if he understood the song. He said his Arabic isn't so strong but he wants to learn. I told him I could teach him. He was confused—how does an American Jew become Israeli and know Syrian Arabic? And why not just Modern Standard Arabic? I explained that I studied with a Syrian professor from Damascus in college—in the United States. He thought I was kidding but then I started speaking to him in Syrian again and he realized I was the real deal. He took my number—I hope he calls and I can connect him to his heritage. You could digest that sentence for a lifetime.

Before I left, I asked the second barista if he understood the song. He could pass for Arab, but it turns out he was Jewish. He said he thought it was about peace. What a beautiful sentiment. In a day and age when many Israelis and Americans would assume the worst of a song in Arabic, this young kid, smack in the middle of Tel Aviv, assumes it's about peace. It just touched my heart.

I told the kids the song was actually about encouraging people to vote in the Egyptian elections. I explained some of the verses and they were eager to learn.

So here we were—three Jews, one Ashkenazi American, one Syrian, and one from who knows where. Sitting in Israel, listening to Egyptian music, babbling in a mixture of Hebrew and Arabic.

If there's one thing I can take from today, it's that where Jewish starts and Arab ends isn't so clear. Just like the bilingual script in my banner photo. When coming to Israel, the absolute best thing you can do is to leave your assumptions at the door. And the second-best thing you can do is to learn a language so filled with love and art and history that you'll be bursting at the seams making new friends from every race and religion. And that language, my friends, is Arabic.

EATING BAKLAVA WITH A PALESTINIAN

PlantingRootsBearingFruits.com, July 26, 2017

THIS IS GOING TO BE REALLY HARD TO SUMMARIZE IN A BLOG, BUT I'M GOING to give it a go.

Tonight, I had baklava with a Palestinian.

On an evening stroll in Yafo, I stopped by the Abouelafia bakery. It's a renowned Middle Eastern bakery that attracts people of all faiths and backgrounds. As I like to do, I started speaking Arabic with a middle-aged gentleman working there named Adnan.

Since we're in the Middle East, instead of exchanging pleasantries and saying "nice to meet you", I invited him to sit down with me and we talked for about two hours. Also important to add that this conversation was fueled by lots of baklava and *knafeh* [79]. And it was delicious.

First things first—Adnan is a cool guy. He helped me hand-pick the best baklava (there were easily two dozen kinds). He put on Nancy Ajram[80] for me. He told me I spoke great Arabic. He's even letting me come back and pay him tomorrow since I didn't realize they were cash-only. Because that's what we do here.

We talked about everything. Bibi[81] (we both don't like him). Abu Mazen[82] (we both don't like him). Hamas[83] (we both don't like them). And politicians in general (we both don't really like them).

We also talked about the shared history of Arabs and Jews, as carriers of two of the world's oldest civilizations. Our shared linguistic heritage (Hebrew and Arabic are both Semitic languages). Our love of learning.

I told him how half of the students in my college Arabic class were Jewish and that many spoke Hebrew, so when the Arabic professor started speaking on the first day, many Jews were laughing and nodding along with him. And the non-Jewish students were totally confused. Because Jews and Arabs have a shared cultural heritage.

Then we delved deeper into politics. First, he said that he has no problem with Jews. Jews and Arabs are regular people who just want to eat, sleep, drink, educate their children, and live a happy life. He said his family's neighbors back in 1948 (before Israel's independence) were Jewish. His family is from East Jerusalem.

East Jerusalem. We could unpack that phrase for literally eons and still be talking. So, let's sum it up—in 1948, Israel's Arab neighbors invaded the nascent country. Israel won its independence and the parts of the U.N. mandate that were supposed to be a new Arab country were annexed by Egypt (the Gaza Strip) and Jordan (the West Bank). Jerusalem was divided, with the western part in Israeli hands and eastern part in Jordanian hands. In 1967, when Israel's neighbors again tried to invade, they were rebuffed, and Israel won Gaza and the West Bank, including East Jerusalem, home to many Jewish, Muslim, and Christian holy sites.

While Israel never formally annexed the West Bank and Gaza Strip, it did so with East Jerusalem. The political reasons are complex, but part of the rationale was that Jerusalem was Israel's (now unified) capital and home to the holiest site in Judaism—the Temple Mount[84]. Under Jordanian rule, Jewish holy sites were neglected or destroyed and Israelis weren't allowed to visit them.

The point of this isn't to rehash history or to debate politics. It's to say that since Adnan is from East Jerusalem, he is different from other Arab citizens of Israel. Arab-Israelis who live in pre-1967 Israel are full voting citizens and variously identify as Arab-Israelis, Arabs, Israelis, Palestinians, or Palestinian-Israelis. More often than not in public discourse, they are referred to as Arab-Israelis, though people's personal identifications may vary.

Folks from East Jerusalem, however, are largely permanent residents, which entitles them to many government services including healthcare. They are eligible to apply for citizenship if they renounce foreign citizenships, which is a complicated issue involving national identity and bureaucratic red tape.

Going back to the story, Adnan tells me that even though he had Israeli citizenship, since he spent seven years abroad working in Romania (which, incidentally, is where some of my family lived before immigrating to America), when he tried to return to Israel, they told him he had lost his citizenship. Even though he was born in Jerusalem and his family has lived there for who knows how many generations.

Eventually he got Romanian citizenship, came back, and then through a process of waiting for three years in Israel without being able to travel abroad, he became a citizen again.

I've tried to avoid writing about the Israeli-Arab conflict on this blog because I'm sick and tired of people thinking that's the only thing that's going on in this region. There's a lot of life and beauty here and I can't think of a single friend who visited China showing concern over the plight of Tibetans (which they should—they're being violently oppressed by the Chinese government). The point is I want my journey to be about so much more than that—and I'm tired of the media turning both Israelis and Palestinians into monkeys for the world to watch while other countries deteriorate without notice.

And the conflict is here. You can't totally avoid it, no matter what you do. It landed on my lap because I talked to a guy at a bakery for goodness sakes.

I've spoken to many Arab-Israelis in Yafo and had a great time. Things aren't always great for them either, but they're pretty good. I spent 30 minutes the other day in a McDonald's talking to an Arab-Israeli girl who's going to an Anime convention in Ramat Gan and speaks perfect Arabic, Hebrew, and English (in addition to the Japanese she's learning). If she lives abroad in Japan, she won't lose her citizenship, thank God.

But Adnan is not an Arab-Israeli. He's a Palestinian (in his own words). He's a Palestinian with Israeli residency, caught between a right-wing Israeli government and the absolute insanity that is Palestinian politics. He lives in a place claimed by two peoples and on some level, isn't allowed to really fully be a part of either.

I am proud to have made *aliyah*. *Aliyah* in Hebrew means "rising up". It is not just immigration. It is a process by which a Jew returns to the Holy Land to live with his or her people. It is an adventure and a blessing. I am grateful to the Israeli people and the Israeli government for giving me the opportunity of a lifetime.

Adnan's a great guy and also has some problematic and contradictory thinking. He doesn't like Zionists and likes Jews (a whole lot of us are Zionists, especially here). He said that Arabs have always treated Jews well historically and that hasn't always been true.[85] When he went to get his citizenship back, he ridiculed the Ethiopian-Israeli at the embassy saying she didn't look like she was from Israel.

The point is not to make Adnan out to be some idealized perfect person or some terrible anti-Semitic monster. He's a complicated person with a good heart. The point of *aliyah* is to rise up. I have a right to be here. Jews have a right to be here and to protect ourselves from harm. And Arabs–Palestinians–have a right to be here, too.

I will use my *aliyah* to lift myself and my people up. And I will use it to lift up Palestinians like Adnan who lose their citizenship when moving abroad while I gain mine for moving here.

If my government can support me in building a new life here, surely it can let Adnan keep his dignity. Those are my Jewish values.

A TALE OF TWO JEWS

PlantingRootsBearingFruits.com, October 22, 2017

Peki'in[86] is a beautiful Druze[87] village in the north of Israel. Or, should I say, a Druze and Jewish village.

This picturesque town is filled with delicious Syrian-style food you can literally eat out of a family's kitchen. The Arabic of the villagers mingles with the Hebrew of the tourists.

What you might not know is that Jews are not just visitors to this town. Peki'in is the site of a Jewish community that has continuously lived there since the destruction of the Temple in Jerusalem 2,000 years ago. It's something I knew little about when I arrived—and learned a lot about when I visited.

My first glimpse into the Jewish past of this town was that there's a rabbi's cave. What is a rabbi's cave? Well Rabbi Shimon Bar Yochai[88] (Rashbi) was hiding from the Romans in 70 C.E., who forbade the study of Torah. So he came to this cave and hid to keep his traditions—our traditions—alive. It's utterly fascinating how every corner of this land is filled with my history.

Here are his digs and a taste of the town:

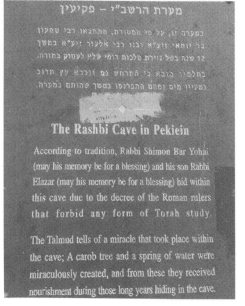

מערת הרשב"י – פקיעין

The Rashbi Cave in Pekiein

According to tradition, Rabbi Shimon Bar Yohai (may his memory be for a blessing) and his son Rabbi Elazar (may his memory be for a blessing) hid within this cave due to the decree of the Roman rulers that forbid any form of Torah study.

The Talmud tells of a miracle that took place within the cave; A carob tree and a spring of water were miraculously created, and from these they received nourishment during those long years hiding in the cave.

After this delightful Jewish surprise, my friend and I headed to eat Druze food out of the backyard of a man's home. This is not a restaurant—there is no menu. There is delicious food that they bring you from their home kitchen, you eat, and then you pay. And mostly you moan in pleasure the whole time as you devour delicious salads, fresh pita, and meat.

I had a great time talking with the Druze family in Arabic. Not only is our Arabic very close (I learned the Syrian dialect and most Israeli Druze migrated to present-day Israel from Syria), but I felt very affirmed by them Jewishly. For example, an old Druze woman (in Hebrew) wished me a Rosh Hashanah[89] sweeter than apples and honey. The Druze people know the Jewish holidays, they respect Jewish holy sites, they frankly just love Jews. Given all the traumas that Jews have experienced—and the subsequent sectarian bitterness that can come between us—I sometimes feel safer as a Jew with Druze than as a Jew with Jews!

Thinking I had finished my adventure, I came across two elderly women. I thought both were Druze. But one woman—in Druze Arabic—tells me she's Jewish. Say what? She then tells me (again, this is all in Arabic) that there is a synagogue in the town built at the time of the destruction of the Temple[90] in Jerusalem 2,000 years ago.

She grabbed her keys and said she'd open it for me.

At this point, Jewish tourists started crowding around us as I explained what was going on in Hebrew. We headed to the synagogue and lo and behold—there is one. And inside, she explains, are fragments from Jerusalem at the time of the Temple—maybe even from the Temple itself. I didn't take pictures because it was the Sukkot holiday and even though nobody was praying, I felt it was disrespectful.

But man, was it awesome. I gingerly asked her if I could touch one of the menorah-shaped stones from the time of the Temple. She said of course.

And so I touched the stones my ancestors carved 2,000 years ago. I've never felt so connected to my past—or to the reasons I came to live here. Judaism is not a metaphor in Israel—it is both past and present. I brought my soul home to where it came from. I think my ancestors would be proud.

Still in awe of this experience (and having had the chance to climb to the roof of the synagogue, which was also cool), I strolled down the street. A man sat on his porch and we started to talk. At first we talked in Hebrew, and then in Druze Arabic. Turns out he's from the same family as the elderly woman who let me into the synagogue.

And, of course, because "two Jews, three opinions", they don't talk! The man's family had left the village for a few years because they were uncertain what might happen in Israel's War of Independence. They feared that the Arab armies might kill them. So as a child, he moved with several other Peki'in families to the Israeli city of Hadera. He told me how as a kid, since his native tongue was Arabic, he often felt afraid to talk lest the other kids think he was the "enemy". So he learned Hebrew in school and spoke Arabic at home.

As an adult, he chose to return to Peki'in to look after his family's lands. And due to who knows what kind of internal politics involving the Jewish Agency and the village synagogue etc. etc., he and the old woman down the street—the only other Jew in town—don't talk.

Sometimes, there are valid reasons not to talk to others. I know this from having dealt with toxic relatives myself. That being said, there's something about this story that just disturbs me.

You've got a community of Jews who despite invader after invader, after massacre after persecution, managed to remain present in the land of Israel for 2,000 years. And yet, the last two Jews there just can't make it work.

Here's my thought: Peki'in is a beautiful town. If you haven't gone, stop going to the same goddamn bar in Tel Aviv and get off your ass and visit your past. The air will fill your soul and you can just be in the moment. No yoga needed.

And if you're a Jew, remember the lesson of Peki'in. Diversity is good, survival is crucial, and so is tolerance. If we get to a place where we're so few yet so divided, how will we ever move forward? Extend the olive branch, step outside your bubble, and show your neighbor some love.

If we can't learn it from ourselves, then learn it from the Druze. Love your neighbor as yourself. Always with kippah[91], sometimes with one, or without one. Secular, Reform, Orthodox. In Arabic. In Hebrew. In your heart.

HITCHHIKING ON A
DRUZE GOLF CART

PlantingRootsBearingFruits.com, September 9, 2017

TONIGHT WAS ROUGH. I HAD AN AMAZING SHABBAT WHICH INCLUDED hosting American students, Reform services, Libyan food, the beach, and an Israeli techno party. After all that, I headed to an "American-style" restaurant in Tel Aviv only to find all sorts of Trump-themed and racist paraphernalia. It was an unwelcome surprise for someone who came here to get away from that. I felt angry and typecast. The only good part was my excellent company and the mac n' cheese. I headed home feeling deflated and wondering why I was here. It's hard to be a Jew in America and it's hard to be American in Israel.

After blowing off some steam, I decided to write about my trip to Daliat Al Karmel and Haifa. Because there, I felt the inspiration that can happen in Israel.

Let's start in Daliat Al Karmel. A beautiful Druze village, I loved exploring every nook and cranny. I had heard there was a monastery nearby, so I made my way by foot. Each person I asked for directions told me it was five minutes away. I asked four people the same question, so needless to say it was more than five minutes away. After 30-40 minutes in the heat, I saw a golf cart heading towards me. I asked the man and his son in Arabic for a lift—and so I hitchhiked with the Druze family to the monastery.

This place is gorgeous. On top of the roof, you can see all of Israel's North. It looks like this:

I felt at peace. Tel Aviv is a disgusting dirty city. It's a fun place. It's filled with youth and queer people and the beach and a million and a half cultures. But it's gross. And loud. The North is peaceful. It is where I go to meditate and connect with God.

Realizing I was far away from the village bus and in need of a way home, I talked to the Druze guy who worked at the front desk. Since this is Israel, there is ALWAYS a solution. A priest from the monastery was headed back to Haifa, where I was staying.

I ran after his car and hopped in. The generous and kind Italian priest drove me the entire 45-minute ride. He spoke decent Spanish and I speak

Spanish so we talked that way—in "Itañol" as he called it. He works for a Roman Catholic church in Haifa that cooperates with Greek Catholics and Maronites—both of whom are also in communion with Rome. He loves life in Israel and wants to stay. He even did an ulpan—although he was frustrated that the teacher only explained things in Russian! Twenty-five percent of Haifa is Russian so it makes sense. Kind of funny that the words he learned in ulpan were *zdrastvootie* and *pazhalsta*.

I then went out in Haifa to check out the nightlife. I connected with some Americans teaching English in Haifa, which was great. It's nice to get a dose of the motherland once in a while. I was then headed home when I heard Arabic music blasting from a sushi bar. I immediately went inside and found an entirely Arab sushi restaurant singing and dancing. I joined in, started clapping and dancing. It was hands down the most fun I'd had since arriving in Israel. And there wasn't a fellow Jew in sight. Because it would probably never occur to a Sabra to step foot in this place. I'm pretty fearless and open-minded, so I said what the hell.

The next thing I knew, the music stopped and the bartender started belting out some amazing Arabic tunes. And he. was. GOOD. Everyone started swinging and swaying and banging on the bar.

At 3:30 a.m. I headed home. I couldn't help but think now how my Americanness helped make these moments possible. My multilingual interactions. My trust of Druze and Arabs. My appreciation for all religious traditions.

Because my American identity isn't a metaphor. And it's not a Britney Spears concert or a goofy picture of Donald Trump or a selfie in Times Square.

It's my appreciation for diversity. My willingness to listen. My open-mindedness and my love for my neighbors—Muslim, Christian, Jewish, Hindu, Buddhist, you name it.

When I made *aliyah*, some Sabras told me not to hang out too much with other Americans. Not to be too diasporic.

Bullshit. My American identity makes me a better Israeli. Quite a number of Jews here speak better German than Arabic and know more about Berlin than Kafr Qasem[92].

I intend to be part of the solution here as an American-Israeli. Instead of throwing shade, hop on the golf cart with me. We'll climb atop a monastery in the middle of nowhere. We'll stare out at the North and realize that anything is possible if you just let yourself dream. The American-Israeli dream.

A GOOD GUY FROM NAZARETH

PlantingRootsBearingFruits.com, May 6, 2018

Today was Lebanon's first election in nine years. One of the reasons I learned Arabic as a teenager was because I grew up with a Lebanese friend, Jad. I've written about him before[93]. He passed away[94] too young.

I often feel his spirit here in Israel. When I was in high school, I would go over to his family's house and eat their pistachio candies like a madman. When I started learning Arabic at the Jewish Community Center in high school, he and his mom would help teach me. I still remember her telling me the difference between *jiddan* and *katheeran*. And I remember him laughing his ass off when I first tried to say *khalass*. I say it better now, man. ☺

Jad's family is unique—half Syrian, half Lebanese. Half Muslim, half Christian. With many Jewish friends in the U.S. I even remember his mom telling me once that sometimes when she sees Israelis, she can't tell them apart from Lebanese people. And she's right, as I discovered when I hit on a guy here who looked like David Goldstein but turned out to be Muhammad Abbas[95].

At a time when the world seems increasingly polarized between religions and political parties, Jad's example reminds me that for every depressing news story, there's a complex and welcoming person not making the front pages. An example I strive to recall living in the beautiful, complicated pressure cooker I call home.

For those of you who don't know, because I'm an Israeli citizen, I can't go to Lebanon. Israeli law and Lebanese law both forbid it. Even though there is no other Arab city I'd rather visit than Beirut, I can't right now. And may never be able to. Which is so, so sad.

The closest I can get is northern Israel. Where the food smells like Jad's kitchen and the Arabic sounds like his parents' friends chatting on the back veranda.

So I headed north.

You see, Lebanese elections aren't a trivial matter for us. While I can't recall a single American who gave a shit about Mexico's elections (though they should), Lebanese elections matter a lot for Israel. Because we're teetering on the brink of a potential war between a Sunni-Israeli-American axis versus Iran, Syria, and Hezbollah. The latter an actual Lebanese political party determined to wipe Israel off the face of the planet.

So, this is no suburban mayoral election in Kansas. This *matters*. In a way few Americans can understand. Right now, there's a coalition government between Hezbollah and the more Sunni/Christian/Western-oriented parties. If there are some strange surprises in the results, who knows what will happen in the region. All we need is a spark, and…kaboom.

It's hard to live with that over your head, yet Israelis—both Arab and Jewish—are amazing at it. While I see my American friends agonizing on Facebook over what color to paint their apartments or how to answer an email, my Israeli friends are traveling to Thailand, are partying, are holding Jewish-Arab dialogue groups, and strive to squeeze every last bit of juice out of life. Perhaps when you have a sense of your own fragility and our inability to control certain things (i.e. foreign elections or terrorists or the weather), you can choose to just let go and live. And stop worrying about inconsequential shit and start living in the reality that is not knowing what tomorrow will bring. To your benefit.

So I intended to head towards the Lebanese border—maybe Rosh Hanikra or the Christian village of Fassouta—but the weather was cloudy. So I figured, with a bit of Jad's inspiration, that the view could wait. And instead, I was able to meet up with a friend for dinner at an Ethiopian Jewish restaurant in Haifa. (Which was delightful—Hanevi'im 20 down the stairs, you won't regret it.)

Afterwards, we ate *the* most delicious *knafeh*[96] I've had in my life. And I've been to dozens of Arab villages all over the country. It was personalized and freshly baked for us like a pizza. I've never eaten something so delicious.

I wanted to speak some Arabic today. In the back of my head, I wanted to hear what people thought about the Lebanese elections. But honestly, I'm just as happy to speak the language with good people.

The guy behind the counter was more than happy to chat. He was excited to hear my Syrian accent[97] and puzzled as to how I got it. Ahmed told me he's from Nazareth. I told him about my visit there and asked if there were Christian and Muslim neighborhoods (it's a mixed city). His answer was telling: "We're not racist. We all live together, Muslims and Christians, and I like Jews too. We all have one God."

I joked, "Well, except for Hindus; they have many." He laughed. ☺

He told me: "Some Muslims and Christians even marry each other."

I was surprised. There's very little marriage across religious lines in Israel—in any direction. And truth be told there are tensions in Nazareth. I wondered if it was accepted. He said not necessarily, but it happens. And he said it with a smile because he says he sees no problem with it.

I told him I'm gay, and was recently in a Druze village[98], and maybe I'd date a Druze guy. I paused for a second and added: "Or I dunno, maybe a Christian or Muslim one. Do you know someone?"

He laughed and said he didn't. And I added: "That you know of. Maybe they're afraid to say it." And, to my great delight, he nodded and said: "You might be right."

And that he'd keep his eyes peeled for me.

I have no idea what's going on in Lebanon right now. Looks like half the populace didn't even vote because their politicians are just as dumb as ours or America's or anywhere else.

What I do know is Jad's spirit is not across the border, it's not in the news, and it's not at a ballot box.

It's in the smile Ahmed and I shared. The love of humanity and the willingness to learn and to overcome the fear instilled in us by fanatics.

If you want to boil down my country—and our neighbors—into a bunch of statistics or boycotts or black-and-white thinking—go ahead. Live in a world full of judgment so far from reality and you will both suffer and create suffering.

I prefer to meet people like Ahmed. Just an open-minded Muslim guy from Nazareth hanging out in Hebrew and Arabic with an American-Israeli gay Jew. Over the best dessert I've ever eaten.

Some people say Jesus was a great guy from Nazareth. But the one I know is named Ahmed.

P.S. My banner photo is of street art reminding us about the train that used to run from Beirut to Haifa[99]. May I live to ride such a train again.

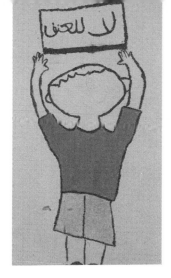

AND THAT'S HOW I LEARNED
THE ARABIC WORD FOR "TERROR ATTACK"

PlantingRootsBearingFruits.com, November 1, 2017

IN A HORRIFIC TERRORIST ATTACK IN NEW YORK, EIGHT PEOPLE WERE KILLED[100] and at least another dozen were wounded. I found out about the attack while perusing Facebook in an ice cream parlor in Yafo. Everyone around me was laughing and having a good time and I just froze and started checking in on all my friends. My emotions welled up as I saw 37 friends were marked safe. Thank God. And then I was on the verge of tears as I noticed that 175 friends of mine had not yet confirmed their status. I even noticed some people had had friends ask them if they were safe and had not responded yet.

I then started messaging friends frantically, trying to find out if they were okay. This is the strange and challenging part of being a dual citizen—I'm feeling the pain of my friends in America while I'm sitting at a gelato shop and people are giggling. Obviously not at what happened, but they just don't know what's going on. It's somewhat of a dual life.

I finally found out a close friend was safe—but her husband works very close to the attack. Thank God he survived, but it's scary to think about. Unfortunately for Israelis, this isn't a new concept, although it's one Israeli experience I hope to never have to suffer.

As I write this blog, it's still Halloween in America. Halloween in Israel is weird—it's almost non-existent. Some of the things I love about the holiday, like picking pumpkins, hayrides, pumpkin pie, candy corn, seeing cute kids in costume, or going to a friend's party—they just don't happen that much here. It's not part of the culture. Understandable, but I still miss it. It's doubly hard because one of my very toxic relatives has a birthday on Halloween so it brings up all sorts of mixed emotions.

Tonight, I didn't expect a scary Halloween, but I got one. Just like the Halloweens with some of my relatives and just like all too many days that have scarred people in the Land of Israel.

Some people ask me how I get through the tough times, through the excruciating challenges that I face as an *oleh chadash*, as a new Israeli citizen. You know how? Everyday miracles.

Before I heard about the attack, I was talking with an adorable 17-year-old named Tony who worked at the ice cream shop. He really likes American rap, so I suggested some artists (he had never heard of Common[101]!). We talked about how he wants to move to Canada or maybe go to college in Germany to become an engineer. When it came up that I'm gay, his co-worker joked that he's a homophobe or a closet-case (this is the humor here—this is not derogatory). He of course denied it and said he likes everyone. He even was a little self-conscious and asked me if he looked like a homophobe. Of course I told him he doesn't (is there a way to look homophobic?), and he smiled. What a nice young Jewish boy with a *goldene neshamah*—a beautiful soul.

Wrong. Tony is Arab. And like not a small number of Arabs here, if you called him David Goldstein, you'd think he's an American Jew. Once he shared that he was Arab, I switched from Hebrew to Arabic and we kept talking. About music, travel, culture, you name it. After every customer he served, he'd come back and keep talking to me.

After I found out about the attack, I was visibly upset. I didn't say anything because I was too busy checking in on my friends. But eventually I needed to go home and sit in a quiet place where I could call people.

Before leaving, I wanted to tell Tony why I had to go. Many Arabs here mix Hebrew into their Arabic. The Hebrew word for terrorist attack is "*pigua*", and it would not be strange for an Arab to speak in Arabic but simply use a Hebrew word in the middle of a sentence. Much like American Jews sprinkle our English with Yiddish and Hebrew. But I knew that if I spoke with Tony in Arabic and then said the word "*pigua*" in the middle of the sentence, the Jewish customers might flip out and I didn't want to scare anyone.

So I looked at Google Translate to find the Arabic word: "*hujoom*". I told Tony about what happened in New York and that I needed to go home to check in on friends. He looked shocked and then sad. He came over and gave me a nice warm bro handshake. I hope to see him again soon at the ice cream shop—he might not be a nice Jewish boy, but he's certainly a nice Arab boy. And while I hope he pursues his dreams to study abroad, a part of me will be sad that this country will miss out on the presence of a kind person.

And that's how I learned the Arabic word for "attack". Not by, thank God, an attack on me here in Israel. And not from the media. But rather, from seeing my friends in pain in America and wanting to share my sadness with a new friend; an Arab friend. A 17-year-old kid who loves hip-hop and scoops ice cream. My neighbor.

There is nothing positive to take from a terrorist attack. It's murder, plain and simple. It's deranged and it's sad. I hope we can make a world where this kind of hate doesn't exist anymore and we can live in peace. Like my banner photo from a mural I saw in Tarshiha[102] says in Arabic: "No to violence."

In the meantime, let's live. Look for the everyday miracles, like my interaction with Tony. An interaction made possible by my decision as a 17-year-old to start learning Arabic at the Jewish Community Center in Rockville, Maryland. And for three years in college in St. Louis. And with Syrian refugees over Skype. And by his decision to open up to me—to show me kindness, to respect my queer identity, and to show empathy in my time of sorrow.

Peace is not made through powerful men shaking hands. That may be part of it, but it's the opening of hearts that truly sustains it and makes it possible. May we all find a way to do so every day, even just a little bit. It makes our world a better place and it gives us hope to overcome great challenges.

May the memory of those who fell today be for a blessing. May God bring healing to wounded. And may we know the fruits of peace so that the scariest Halloween we have is when our kids sneak up on us and say:

"Boo."

BEDOUIN YIDDISH

Yes, you read that right. We'll get to it—read the whole way through 😊

PlantingRootsBearingFruits.com, January 11, 2018

TODAY, I WENT SOUTH. I'VE EXPLORED A LOT OF ISRAEL'S CENTER AND north—with plenty more to discover. And I've ventured a little south since making *aliyah* to Ashdod. Now was the time to learn about another region.

I hopped on the train and headed to Be'er Sheva. It is a city actually mentioned in the Torah and there's a well there that, according to tradition, was dug by Abraham himself. I wanted to visit, but it's one of the very few places in Israel you need to call in advance!

I visited the city market, which was cool. An amazing diversity of cultures that reminded me a lot of my neighborhood in Tel Aviv. Just with less traffic and yelling. 😊

I went into an electronics store and asked in Arabic where I could buy Bedouin[103] music. For those who are wondering, Bedouin are substantially different in culture, language, and religiosity from many other Arabs in Israel. Therefore, their music is different as well.

The young man made me a deal and custom-burned me a CD with MP3s of *dahiyye* music. It's basically happy Bedouin dance music—take a look[104]. Somewhat reminiscent of the *dabke* I've learned—but in the words of the Bedouin man: "That's *fellahi* music". *Fellahin*[105] were the villagers and farmers of the region, as opposed to the nomadic Bedouin. Most Arabs in Israel today are descendants of *Fellahin* and have distinct dialects from the Bedouin, who speak a bit more like *Fusha*,[106] the standard Arabic which was likely modeled after them.

I was then peppered with questions about why I wasn't married. Lest you think this is only a Bedouin phenomenon, it has been a frequent first question amongst Jews, other Arabs, even Samaritans here. It is extremely difficult for me—as a queer person, as an American (where this is considered invasive), and as a survivor of partner abuse.

Eventually I shrugged it off by saying I was new to the country and needed time to settle in. Having gotten my Bedouin music, I decided to keep exploring.

I then came upon a bona fide music shack. A shack because it looks like one. And bona fide because this man knew his music. No CD burning here. He had hundreds of CDs.

I felt much more at ease here—Ahmed, also Bedouin, was gentle and friendly. And never asked me about my marital status. We bonded over Arabic music as he showed me tons of options. Eventually I bought an Israeli Bedouin CD (with songs from both the north and the south), Syrian dialect music (that's the one I speak!), and another Bedouin CD from a town near Be'er Sheva. I personally find it miraculous to find Syrian-dialect music in a Bedouin shop in Be'er Sheva. First off, most Arabic music is not recorded in Syrian, even when the artists are from there. Egyptian tends to dominate. In addition, ten years ago when I took my Syrian dialect class, I could never have imagined this scenario. And I love it. When the stars align, language and culture bring me closer to good people like Ahmed.

Be'er Sheva's Jewish community is also very diverse. Walking around, I found several Indian and Ethiopian Jewish stores. There were tons of Russian signs. I even found a sign publicizing a concert at a Tunisian synagogue from the famed isle of Djerba[107]—around the corner from the beautiful mural in my banner photo—showing how the ancient and modern co-exist and feed off each other in this beautiful land.

I toured a bit of the Old City, which I hope to return to in particular to see the Grand Mosque/Museum of Islamic and Near Eastern Cultures. Like nearly everything in Israel, this place is not without its controversy. An Ottoman-era building, the mosque is no longer used for prayer, although local Muslims would like to do so. Instead, the city of Be'er Sheva wanted to turn it into a general museum. The Israeli Supreme Court, perhaps weaving between the two, decided it could be a museum[108] but it had to be dedicated to Islamic history. I'm looking forward to visiting, being a fan of Islamic art and history, and would be happy to see it peacefully resume its role as a house of prayer.

Having the desire to see more Bedouin culture, I hopped on a bus and went to Rahat[109]. An entirely Bedouin city, it is a fantastic place to go to experience their culture. Since it was already dark and my transportation options were dwindling to go back home (this can be a stressful part of spontaneous travel), I focused on my goal: food. Before I sat down to eat, though, I met a wonderful young man named Muhammad who is studying English. I had asked him for directions, one thing led to another, and we decided to stay in touch and exchange languages. In particular, I'm dying to learn his Bedouin dialect. And I can help him with English. 😊

I sat down to eat a feast. This is not an exaggeration. For 25 shekels, approximately $7.30, I got to eat this:

The picture doesn't really do it justice- it's huge. I didn't finish half the rice (chicken is buried in it)—and I was very hungry. The bread is delightful—kind of like Druze pita, i.e. nothing like the pita you'd find in a grocery store. The full bowl of soup that came with it was tomato-ey, a little spicy, and delicious. The rice kind of tasted like Biryani[110] for any of my fellow South Asian food fans. And it was covered in peanuts, peas, veggies, and delicious sauce. My doggy-bag was enormous.

The people there were so kind. I have to paint this picture for you— there are zero Jews anywhere. I can't imagine many Jews come to Rahat to dine in one of the Arab restaurants that often sit at the footsteps of their villages for Jews to eat at without going "too far in". I could be wrong, maybe some come. All I can say for sure is that when I was there, I was the only one around. And a totally novel figure.

People were so curious to talk to me. I was asked a million questions (fortunately nothing about marriage). All of them kind and welcoming. We mostly spoke in Arabic. I asked them to teach me some Bedouin—they said I spoke *fellahi*! 😊 We used a few Hebrew words but they truly loved to practice their English. 😊 People knew I was American, Jewish, and Israeli. And I have to say, and this repeatedly shocks me, being American has been a huge plus to my travels in the Middle East. Despite the fact that the American government has a very long history of bullying other countries, so many people here still love America. Jews, Arabs—doesn't matter. It's fascinating and frankly really encouraging. It's also a great way to disarm the people who are, in fact, suspicious of you, because I can play the innocent stranger. To be fair, I pretty much am one. 😊

Before my sated self headed to the bus (and then an exceedingly long train ride because I missed the more direct train—note to self for next trip), a man grabbed my phone and insisted we take a selfie. Apparently some concepts are universal!

As I headed to the bus, a man asked me what languages I spoke. One of them is Yiddish. And in a moment that you couldn't even dream of in the wildest of scenarios, the Bedouin man tells me there's a guy in their town… who speaks Yiddish. In shock and amazement, I asked why. He said that the man, back in the day when Yiddish was more widely spoken here, learned it just as he did every common tongue in the area. My grin, inside and out, could not have been bigger.

In pure cultural ecstasy, I headed home on a very slow train. With a lot of time to digest a rich and exciting day.

Intercultural exploration and communication can be very challenging.

One does not come out of the womb with the skills necessary to make it happen—even if you may have some characteristics that help. I've spent my whole life communicating across cultures. From my early years in Japan to my schooling in Maryland with so many immigrant friends to my work for refugee rights to the dozen or so languages I've studied (eight or nine of which I can currently speak). None of this happened by osmosis nor just because I have "an ear" for it. I do have an ear for it—but just like a concert violinist doesn't magically pick up a bow and play a concerto, I have honed these skills over years of practice and joy.

Today is the kind of day I'm proud to call myself a cultural explorer. One who learns, who tries new things, who makes people smile, who grows, who creates, who makes the world a better place.

If you're looking for new adventure, the world is your backyard. And your backyard just may have a Bedouin Yiddish speaker.

WHEN GOD SPEAKS THROUGH GRAFFITI

PlantingRootsBearingFruits.com, August 20, 2017

LAST NIGHT, I HEARD MY FIRST REALLY RACIST COMMENT IN ISRAEL. SOME people might be surprised at this. Americans might think that people are way more racist here than they are. And Israelis might think I might be deaf. But the reality is, I have heard racist comments here, but this one felt more real. It wasn't just a comment, it was a diatribe and it was backed by a lot of emotion.

The very long story short is I was talking to a young guy, around 30 years old, Israeli Jew of Middle Eastern descent. His entire point of view could be summed up in one comment he made: "Not all Arabs are terrorists, but all terrorists around the world are Arabs."

There are variations of this phrase around the world. Some people replace Arab with Muslim. It is not a uniquely Israeli phrase, as any Google search will show you.

I was disgusted. I vigorously pushed back against his thinking but it didn't change his mind one bit. It didn't matter how many times I explained about non-Arab terrorists in America or Myanmar or Ireland or anywhere else. This guy was inconvincible.

Anyone who knows me knows that my Zionism, that my Jewish identity, that my very way of interacting with the world is predicated on finding something to love in different cultures, not trashing them.

Feeling thoroughly discouraged, today I hung out in Yafo. Yafo is a predominantly Arab town in the Tel Aviv municipality and it has an extensive multicultural history that includes everyone from Jews to ancient Egyptians to Greeks to Arabs. I needed to be with my people—and today, that meant Arabs.

I talked with a new friend Samir at my baklava hangout. A nice guy with mostly Jewish friends and an open mind. Also some delusional thoughts about whether ISIS really attacked Barcelona (because "who are they?"). And he didn't believe that terrorists in the West Bank get paid for their acts (they do[111]). At the same time, he is extremely opposed to Palestinian terrorism and all violence. And also radically not a radical—he said he won't even go to Mecca in Saudi Arabia, even though his religion demands it, because he's so disgusted by their extremist and corrupt government. I left semi-encouraged, though also feeling like there's a lot of work to do here.

I wandered through Yafo eating Palestinian potato chips, hoping that eating a snack from Hebron would help me heal from the turmoil. I decided to head to the sea. I always find some quiet and nature calms my mind. I had been feeling distant from God and spirituality and kind of hopeless. The waves gave me some respite and a connection to the bigger things in life.

Then I noticed the most interesting graffiti. It said in Hebrew "Ramsey loves Natali". To most people, this might just look like an ordinary graffiti. To me, it was absolutely beautiful. First off, Ramsey is an Arabic name and Natali is kind of a universal name, though my guess is this girl is Jewish because the graffiti is written in Hebrew. So most likely a Jewish-Arab romance, which is heartwarming.

And there's much more to it. Almost two years ago, my friend Jad passed away. I grew up with him in Maryland and he was my first Arab friend. I had had other Arab acquaintances at school, but he was the first person I really connected with. I learned a lot from him about his Lebanese culture—and seeing as he grew up in a suburb that's 30% Jewish, he learned a lot about my culture too. I remember him telling me he could understand a lot of the words at our friends' Bar Mitzvahs because of his Arabic. I was so sad to hear of his passing. You can learn more about what his friendship meant to me in a blog I wrote[112] at the time.

Jad's younger brother, who I always remember hanging out with after our soccer games—his name is Ramsey, just like in the graffiti. At a time when I've found it hard to bridge the distance between my past life in America and my current Israeli life, I felt like this graffiti was a spiritual lifeline. A message from God and Jad that hope is found in the most unlikely places.

In my blog after Jad's death, I wrote: "Just as Jad opened my eyes to his culture, I will make an extra effort to advocate for peace and understanding between Jews and Arabs."

I love all cultures and all peoples. There are good and bad individuals (and many in between) everywhere. With every conversation I have, with every blog I write, with every song I sing I am keeping my promise I made to Jad. To find people of good faith, an open heart, and willingness to listen no matter what their background. To laugh with them and to make the world a better place.

I will be the hope this place needs. Join me.

A PALESTINIAN, AN AMERICAN,
AND AN IRAQI WALK INTO A BAKERY

This story is unique to this collection and has never been featured on the blog.

AROUND THE CORNER FROM WHERE I USED TO LIVE, IN SHCHUNAT HATIKVAH, there were three separate Iraqi bakeries on the same street. Run by Iraqi Jews, they all smelled delicious, filled with the aroma of freshly baked Iraqi pita. It's a pita that's quite different from one you might get in a falafel shop. It's larger, rounder, a teeny bit crispy if part of it burned. It would be amazing for making pizza.

There was one Iraqi bakery in particular that I used to go to. I miss it so much. The woman was so friendly and she still spoke Iraqi Judeo-Arabic. An Arabic I could pretty much understand with my nearby Syrian dialect. One time another Iraqi woman came over and started speaking to her in it and the owner shouted out: "He's American and speaks better Arabic than me!" Probably still the highlight of my Arabic career (other than a time in Haifa when an Arab man shouted to another "We have a foreign Arab here!" as he pointed to me—still the greatest compliment I've ever received).

One day, the woman wasn't there and a man was operating the furnace. His name was Idris—an Arab name. I asked where he was from, expecting most likely Yaffo or perhaps a village up North or Jerusalem.

"Gaza."

I actually think I laughed. It must be a joke. The border with Gaza had been closed for years due to conflict with Hamas. While Palestinian workers used to enter Israel with greater frequency, things have died down considerably, especially from Gaza.

He looked stern. "Yes, I am from Gaza." So we started to speak in Arabic and as best I can remember, he spoke with the Gazan dialect. He said he works Monday through Friday then goes home to Gaza on the weekends. I have no idea if that's true—maybe he works under the table, but Gazan he seemed to be. I sure wasn't about to question it after his reaction.

The next time I saw him, he was in a better mood. The Iraqi woman was there with him. And the three of us got to speaking in Arabic. Iraqi Judeo-Arabic, Gazan, and my own Syrian dialect. An Iraqi, a Palestinian, and an American. All talking in the tongue of Maimonides. I think he would have been proud.

It's one of those small moments that makes you hopeful about the world, the Middle East, about life. Because look at how language can bring such different people together. Laughing, joking, overcoming the things that divide us. Arabic was the glue that made our conversation possible. It just wouldn't have been the same if we hadn't had this ancient language as a resource to bind us together.

So there you have it. In the most conservative neighborhood of Tel Aviv, three people from widely different backgrounds shared a laugh. It'll never make *CNN* or *The New York Times*, but it was real. And it reminds me of the power of words, of language, to make a little peace at a time when we all too often feel like we're picking up the pieces.

To hope.

ABOUT THE AUTHOR

MATT ADLER IS A PROUD AMERICAN AND ISRAELI. A NATIVE OF Washington, D.C., Matt lived in the Yad Eliyahu neighborhood of Tel Aviv during the adventures on which this book is based. In addition to Arabic and Hebrew, Matt speaks Spanish, Portuguese, Catalan, French, and intermediate Yiddish. Visit his blog PlantingRootsBearingFruits.com to explore other overlooked aspects of life in Israel.

NOTES

1   https://en.wikipedia.org/wiki/Druze

2   https://www.jpost.com/Israel-News/Farmland-in-flames-as-Gaza-protests-give-rise-to-kite-terrorism-553329

3   https://natakallam.com/

4   https://www.ynetnews.com/articles/0,7340,L-4335235,00.html

5   http://news.gallup.com/poll/1573/twentytwo-percent-nonhispanic-americans-speak-second-language.aspx

6   https://plantingrootsbearingfruits.wordpress.com/2018/05/01/the-bi-curious-druze-boy/

7   https://en.wikipedia.org/wiki/Shas

8   https://en.wikipedia.org/wiki/Goblet_drum

9   https://en.wikipedia.org/wiki/Mizrahi_music

10   https://en.wikipedia.org/wiki/My_Big_Fat_Greek_Wedding

11   https://en.wikipedia.org/wiki/Ashkenazi_Jews

12   https://natakallam.com/

13   https://en.wikipedia.org/wiki/Ovadia_Yosef

14   https://en.wikipedia.org/wiki/Umm_Kulthum

15   https://en.wikipedia.org/wiki/Kibbeh

16   https://en.wikipedia.org/wiki/Sarit_Hadad

17   https://en.wikipedia.org/wiki/Racism_in_Israel#Sephardim_and_Mizrahim_.28Middle_Eastern_and_North_African_Jews.29

18   https://books.google.co.il/books?id=jbLFAAAAQBAJ

19   https://en.wikipedia.org/wiki/Haredi_Judaism

20   https://en.wikipedia.org/wiki/Mizrachi

21   https://en.wikipedia.org/wiki/Yitzhak_Rabin

22   https://en.wikipedia.org/wiki/Dabke

23   https://www.facebook.com/egbaryaanas/videos/1718612928189784/

24   https://en.wikipedia.org/wiki/Rabin_Square

25   https://www.irac.org/equal-status-for-all-jews

26 https://en.wikipedia.org/wiki/Hasidic_Judaism

27 https://en.wikipedia.org/wiki/Kapparot

28 https://en.wikipedia.org/wiki/Haredi_Judaism

29 https://en.wikipedia.org/wiki/Islamic_scarf_controversy_in_France

30 https://en.wikipedia.org/wiki/Sabra_(person)

31 https://en.wikipedia.org/wiki/Ma%27alot-Tarshiha

32 https://en.wikipedia.org/wiki/Mizrahi_music

33 https://www.youtube.com/watch?v=F-bsf2x-aeE

34 http://www.yourdictionary.com/toches

35 https://www.facebook.com/matt.adler.357/
   videos/10101776092268682/

36 http://natakallam.com/

37 https://en.wikipedia.org/wiki/Haredi_Judaism

38 https://en.wikipedia.org/wiki/Shas

39 https://en.wikipedia.org/wiki/Judaeo-Spanish

40 https://plantingrootsbearingfruits.wordpress.com/2017/12/16/
   dugri-lost-in-translation/

41 https://en.wikipedia.org/wiki/Fureidis

42 https://amiraspantry.com/qamar-al-deen-apricot-drink/

43 https://www.jpost.com/Arab-Israeli-Conflict/KKL-JNF-will-sue-
   Hamas-over-damage-from-rockets-incendiary-kites-559215

44 https://en.wikipedia.org/wiki/Shefa-%27Amr

45 https://en.wikipedia.org/wiki/Kanafeh

46 https://en.wikipedia.org/wiki/Purim

47 https://en.wikipedia.org/wiki/Hamantash

48 https://en.wikipedia.org/wiki/Druze

49 https://en.wikipedia.org/wiki/Daliyat_al-Karmel

50 https://en.wikipedia.org/wiki/Kibbeh

51 https://en.wikipedia.org/wiki/Hushpuppy

52 http://www.israelandyou.com/maqam-abu-ibrahim/

53 https://en.wikipedia.org/wiki/Mezuzah

54 https://en.wikipedia.org/wiki/Israel_Defense_Forces

55 https://en.wikipedia.org/wiki/Kaddish#Mourner.27s_Kaddish

56 https://plantingrootsbearingfruits.wordpress.com/2018/01/11/bedouin-yiddish/

57 https://www.youtube.com/watch?v=1RW3nDRmu6k

58 https://plantingrootsbearingfruits.wordpress.com/2018/04/09/a-preview-of-a-terrorist-attack/

59 https://en.wikipedia.org/wiki/Bnei_Brak

60 https://plantingrootsbearingfruits.wordpress.com/2017/10/29/my-first-haredi-hug/

61 https://plantingrootsbearingfruits.wordpress.com/2017/08/29/hasidic-game-of-thrones/

62 https://plantingrootsbearingfruits.wordpress.com/2017/12/05/the-satmar-part-of-town/

63 https://plantingrootsbearingfruits.wordpress.com/2017/08/21/a-gay-reform-jew-goes-to-bnei-brak/

64 https://plantingrootsbearingfruits.wordpress.com/2018/01/18/a-bisl-hassidus-a-bisl-queerus-a-gay-hasidic-day/

65 https://en.wikipedia.org/wiki/Vizhnitz_(Hasidic_dynasty)

66 http://www.nosachteiman.co.il/

67 https://en.wikipedia.org/wiki/Yemenite_Jews

68 https://en.wikipedia.org/wiki/Belz_(Hasidic_dynasty)

69 https://www.youtube.com/watch?v=oSPg0TV6HPg

70 https://en.wikipedia.org/wiki/Zog_nit_keyn_mol

71 https://en.wikipedia.org/wiki/The_Holocaust

72 https://en.wikipedia.org/wiki/Christianity_and_antisemitism

73 https://en.wikipedia.org/wiki/Islam_and_antisemitism

74 https://en.wikipedia.org/wiki/Antisemitism_in_Europe

75 https://en.wikipedia.org/wiki/Mizrahi_Jews

76 https://en.wikipedia.org/wiki/Modern_Orthodox_Judaism

77 https://en.wikipedia.org/wiki/Ad-Dhahiriya

78 https://en.wikipedia.org/wiki/Levantine_Arabic

79 https://en.wikipedia.org/wiki/Kanafeh

80   https://en.wikipedia.org/wiki/Nancy_Ajram

81   https://en.wikipedia.org/wiki/Benjamin_Netanyahu

82   https://en.wikipedia.org/wiki/Mahmoud_Abbas

83   https://en.wikipedia.org/wiki/Hamas

84   https://en.wikipedia.org/wiki/Temple_Mount

85   https://en.wikipedia.org/wiki/
       History_of_the_Jews_under_Muslim_rule

86   https://en.wikipedia.org/wiki/Peki%27in

87   https://en.wikipedia.org/wiki/Druze_in_Israel

88   https://en.wikipedia.org/wiki/Simeon_bar_Yochai

89   https://en.wikipedia.org/wiki/Rosh_Hashanah

90   https://en.wikipedia.org/wiki/Temple_in_Jerusalem

91   https://en.wikipedia.org/wiki/Kippah

92   https://en.wikipedia.org/wiki/Kafr_Qasim

93   https://plantingrootsbearingfruits.wordpress.com/2017/08/20/
       when-god-speaks-through-graffiti/

94   https://culturallycuriousblog.wordpress.com/2015/11/13/
       in-memory-of-my-friend-jad-zakhour/

95   https://plantingrootsbearingfruits.wordpress.com/2017/09/21/
       my-druze-muslim-orthodox-reform-rosh-hashanah/

96   https://en.wikipedia.org/wiki/Kanafeh

97   https://plantingrootsbearingfruits.wordpress.com/2018/05/05/
       the-north-where-my-arabic-can-breathe/

98   https://plantingrootsbearingfruits.wordpress.com/2018/05/01/
       the-bi-curious-druze-boy/

99   https://en.wikipedia.org/wiki/Palestine_Railways

100   http://edition.cnn.com/2017/10/31/us/new-york-shots-fired/index.
       html

101   https://en.wikipedia.org/wiki/Common_(rapper)

102   https://en.wikipedia.org/wiki/Ma%27alot-Tarshiha

103   https://en.wikipedia.org/wiki/Negev_Bedouin

104 https://www.youtube.com/watch?v=kwYAL4P2dcs&
     index-12&t 415r&list-I I ghF6STpzUFLA3lrxdN8NJw

105 https://en.wikipedia.org/wiki/Fellah

106 https://en.wikipedia.org/wiki/Modern_Standard_Arabic

107 https://en.wikipedia.org/wiki/Djerba

108 https://www.haaretz.com/israel-news/high-court-rules-be-er-sheva-
     mosque-to-be-used-as-islamic-museum-1.369278

109 https://en.wikipedia.org/wiki/Rahat

110 https://en.wikipedia.org/wiki/Biryani

111 http://www.timesofisrael.com/
     palestinians-paid-terrorists-1b-in-4-years-knesset-panel-hears/

112 https://culturallycuriousblog.wordpress.com/2015/11/13/
     in-memory-of-my-friend-jad-zakhour/

Made in the USA
Monee, IL
16 October 2020